UNDERSTA
PUBLIC

Gabriele Ganz is Professor of Public Law
at the University of Southampton.

J.A.G. Griffith is Emeritus Professor of
Public Law in the University of London.

Understanding Law
Editor: J.A.G. Griffith

Understanding Contract Law
John Adams and Roger Brownsword

Understanding Criminal Law
C.M.V. Clarkson

Understanding Public Law
Gabriele Ganz

Understanding Equity and Trusts
Jeffrey Hackney

Understanding Tort Law
Carol Harlow

Understanding Property Law
W.T. Murphy and Simon Roberts

Gabriele Ganz

UNDERSTANDING
PUBLIC LAW

Fontana Press

First published in 1987 by Fontana Paperbacks
8 Grafton Street, London W1X 3LA

Set in 10 point Times

Made and printed in Great Britain
by William Collins Sons & Co. Ltd, Glasgow

Contents

Contents

Editor's Preface

This series is directed primarily at two groups of readers: the general reader who wishes to understand what it is that lawyers are talking about and the law student who is told that he is about to study a subject called tort, or contract, or criminal law, or property, or trusts and equity, or public law. These titles convey little that is clear about the nature of their subjects and the extra-legal meanings that attach to some – such as contract or criminal law – may be misleading.

Each book in this series seeks to explain what the subject is about, what are the special kinds of problems it seeks to solve, and why it has developed as it has. The books are not at all meant to be summaries of their subjects, each of which covers a complicated area of human activity.

The law student will, in his or her course, be expected to read much longer and fuller texts on the subjects, to attend lectures and tutorials. The books in this series seek to provide introductions to be read early in the course or before it begins. It is hoped that these introductions will enable the student to grasp the essentials before coming to grips with the details. So also, the general reader who wishes to pursue the subject more fully will have to read the more detailed texts.

Although these books are intended to be introductions, they are not meant to be simplifications. These are not 'easy' books, however clearly they are written. Understanding law is not an easy matter. This is not, as is often said, primarily because lawyers use words with special meanings. It is because law has to deal with the complications, both personal and commercial, that people become involved in. We are all as busy as ants, more purposeful and sometimes less efficient. Law tries to regularize these complications and so cannot avoid being itself complicated.

Editor's Preface

The intention of the series will be achieved if the books give the reader a broad perspective and a general understanding of the legal principles on which these different subjects are based.

John Griffith
April 1987

Introduction

The British constitution used to be the envy of the world. The Westminster model was one of our main exports – now foreign institutions swell our growing range of imports. Great constitutional writers such as Bagehot (1867) and Dicey (1885) had no doubt that our constitution was superior to the American and French models. Today it is difficult to find any writer who is not critical of our institutions. There is hardly any element of the constitution which has not come under attack. Even the Queen or, more accurately, the functions she may still have to perform – i.e. choosing the Prime Minister and dissolving Parliament – have been subjected to much critical analysis in the light of the possibility of a hung Parliament. Lord Hailsham, when in opposition, condemned the system in its entirety as an 'Elective Dictatorship' and wanted to start afresh with a new constitution (Hailsham, 1976). Roy Jenkins in his Dimbleby lecture 'Home Thoughts from Abroad' laid all our ills at the feet of our electoral system and recommended proportional representation as a panacea (Jenkins, 1979). Richard Crossman (1975), Tony Benn (1980), John Mackintosh (1977) as well as others have pinpointed Prime Ministerial power as the root of all evil. Crossman and Benn have also been in the forefront of the attack on the Civil Service as usurpers of the power of elected governments. Since the Conservatives came to office, criticism has been augmented from the opposite end of the political spectrum which has been reinforced as a result of the leaks of information by Sarah Tisdall and Clive Ponting. The atrophy of the convention of ministerial responsibility to Parliament has been debated since the resignation of Sir Thomas Dugdale over the Crichel Down fiasco. The breakdown of collective responsibility of ministers was documented by the Franks review of the Falkland Islands (Cmnd 8787, 1983) and highlighted by the resignation of Michael Heseltine in the Westland Helicopters affair.

Introduction

The functioning of Parliament has been under constant attack. Reform of the House of Lords has been on the political agenda all this century and abolition has been the official policy of the Labour Party. The working of the House of Commons, especially in the areas of legislation and control over finance, in spite of numerous reforms since the war is still regarded by its own members as in need of drastic change.

The secrecy of governments and in particular the Official Secrets Act 1911, section 2, are almost universally execrated, and the call for a Freedom of Information Act becomes stronger every day. Similarly there has been much pressure for a Bill of Rights to safeguard the rights of the individual against encroachment by the government and Parliament. Carried to its logical conclusion this would challenge the sovereignty of Parliament, the cornerstone of the constitution. It would also involve the judiciary in political decision-making to a much greater degree than at present. The judiciary have not escaped attack for their more active role in controlling the power of public authorities.

The functioning of public authorities and in particular their relationship with each other – i.e. central-local relations and those between the government and nationalized industries – has ranged from a lack of harmony to complete breakdown in the case of some local authorities.

In the past decade or so referenda have been used twice to defuse constitutional issues and have been called for, unsuccessfully so far, to solve other constitutional problems.

The above is not a happy catalogue. Why is almost every aspect of our constitution under attack? Why is it no longer regarded as a model to be copied but as a disaster to be avoided? Is it the institutions which have changed or the people who work them or the people who are governed by them or the circumstances in which they operate? Has economic decline brought about political decline or vice versa? Has the very strength of our unwritten constitution become its weakness? Have the internal conventional safeguards broken down and should they be replaced by a written constitution containing legal safeguards? How could such a change be reconciled with representative democracy? Does such a system of government itself lead to elective dictatorship unless it is restrained by non-elected bodies? Or is our constitution not democratic enough? Should there be more participation by citizens in decision-making, e.g. by referenda, and more openness without which intelligent participation is impossible? Proportional representation would bring a closer correlation between votes and elected representatives. These approaches starting from opposite premises would each lead to a dilution of governmental power. The limits within which governmental power should be constrained is the ultimate question for any constitution. Whether these limits should be external or internal, legal or conventional is a question of means towards this end. Whether the constraints should be democratic or undemocratic is a question of ideology. Constitutional questions cannot be divorced from ideology. It is ideology which determines the content of the constitution. A constitution embodies an ideology, but in an unwritten constitution such as ours there is much flexibility. The same institutions, e.g. the Monarchy, can evolve to serve different ends, and those who work the institutions have much scope to mould them to their own ends, e.g. the Prime Minister.

A constitution cannot be divorced from the social and economic context in which it operates. Depending on these circumstances it may be subjected to strains and conflicts which test it to breaking point. A constitution cannot by itself solve social and economic problems though it may provide the mechanisms for their solution. No constitution can forestall an oil crisis but it can help to mitigate the problems arising therefrom. Economics and politics overlap but they are not coterminous.

All these issues underlie a discussion of the constitution as it exists today. Such a discussion is as difficult as taking a snapshot of a changing panorama or trying to hit a moving target because the subject matter is constantly evolving, sometimes imperceptibly. All constitutions must be able to change if they are not to break and written constitutions usually provide special procedures for this purpose. Our constitution, which is not embodied in one or more documents, is more flexible than almost any other for two reasons. First, so far as it is embodied in legal rules, these can be changed by an Act of Parliament in the same way that any other law can be changed. Secondly, the essence of the British constitution lies not in its laws but in its conventions, i.e. in rules which do not have the force of law but which have evolved gradually and continue to do so and have transformed the constitution behind the legal facade. These two hallmarks of the constitution, the sovereignty of Parliament and the conventions of the constitution, have not escaped the wave of criticism but have been central targets for the attackers. Lord Hailsham put sovereignty of Parliament in the forefront of his indictment because Parliament is 'absolute and unlimited'. This led him to call for legal limits in a written constitution. Similarly the breakdown of conventions relating to the conduct of the Prime Minister, other ministers, the Civil Service and the relationship between central and local government has led to calls by Lord Scarman (1985) for a written constitution as a remedy. These attacks are aimed at the twin pillars of the constitution which must now be evaluated.

1

Elective Dictatorship

The extent to which the perception of the British constitution has changed over the last hundred years is well illustrated by quotations from Dicey's *Law of the Constitution* (1885) and Lord Hailsham's lecture 'Elective Dictatorship' (1976). First, Dicey on sovereignty: 'The essential property of representative government is to produce coincidence between the wishes of the sovereign and the wishes of the subjects. . . . This, which is true in its nature of all real representative government, applies with special truth to the English House of Commons' (p. 84). On conventions, Dicey said: 'The conventions of the constitution now consist of customs which (whatever their historical origin) are at the present day maintained for the sake of ensuring the supremacy of the House of Commons, and ultimately, through the elective House of Commons, of the nation' (pp. 430–1). Contrast these quotations with Lord Hailsham, 'So the sovereignty of Parliament has increasingly become, in practice, the sovereignty of the Commons, and the sovereignty of the Commons has increasingly become the sovereignty of the government, which in addition to its influence in Parliament, controls the party whips, the party machine and the civil service. This means that what has always been an elective dictatorship in theory, but one in which the component parts operated, in practice, to control one another, has become a machine in which one of those parts has come to exercise a predominant influence over the rest' (p. 497). And more succinctly: 'The government controls Parliament and not Parliament the government' (p. 496). So the nub of the indictment is that the elected part of Parliament, namely the House of Commons, having achieved supremacy over the unelected parts, namely the Queen and the House of Lords, has surrendered its sovereignty to the government which controls it through the party machine.

Which of these snapshots represents a more accurate picture of the constitution as it exists today? If the aim of representative government is 'to produce coincidence between the wishes of the sovereign and the wishes of the subjects' the representative body must reflect the wishes of the electorate and exercise control over the government. The crucial issues, therefore, are the electoral system and the relationship between the government and Parliament.

ELECTORAL SYSTEM

Every British citizen aged eighteen years or over who is not serving a sentence of imprisonment and is not a peer is eligible to be placed on the electoral register in a constituency (Representation of the People Act 1983). Normally this involves residence in the constituency on a certain day (10 October) but members of the armed forces and now British citizens who live abroad but have been registered within the previous five years can be entered on the register (Representation of the People Act 1985). At the moment there are 650 constituencies, the boundaries being drawn by impartial Boundary Commissions whose recommendations need the approval of both Houses of Parliament (Parliamentary Constituencies Act 1986). Their impartiality has not prevented their recommendations being highly controversial as the way the boundaries are drawn can profoundly affect the electoral prospects of a particular party. The parties draw their support from different sections of the electorate and the exclusion or inclusion of a particular area can turn a safe seat into a marginal one and vice versa. In 1969 the Labour government refused to implement the Boundary Commissions' recommendations and in 1983 unsuccessfully challenged them in court (*R v. Boundary Commission for England ex parte Foot*, 1983).

Not only the delimitation of boundaries but the choice of candidates by the parties profoundly affects the extent to which the voters' wishes are reflected in the House of Commons because the voter can only choose between rival candidates. Unlike the USA where in some states voters through primaries have a voice in choosing between the parties' candidates, each party here has its own method for choosing candidates. The Labour Party in 1980 insisted that all Labour MPs must undergo a reselection process if they wished to be candidates at the next General Election. Anyone can form a political party, as happened in 1981 when the Social Democratic Party (SDP) was launched. Though election law puts strict limits on expenditure during an election campaign, to prevent bribery and corruption, it is very expensive to fight an election, particularly as national propaganda does not count towards election expenses. The Labour and Conservative parties draw their financial support mainly from the trade unions and industry respectively. The other parties have no such firm financial base and to that extent suffer a considerable electoral disadvantage.

Their main disadvantage is, however, the British electoral system. Electors vote in their constituency and whichever candidate obtains most votes is elected an MP, even if he or she obtains only one vote more than his or her nearest rival and only a small percentage of the total vote. This system works best when there are only two parties, though even then it is possible for a party to obtain more votes over the country as a whole but have fewer seats in the House of Commons because its support may be unevenly distributed, so that it obtains big majorities in some seats and loses narrowly in others. This result is accentuated when there are three or more parties. A third party like the Liberals or now the Social Democratic and Liberal Alliance, whose support is spread fairly evenly throughout the country, is likely to win few seats but come second in many. Thus in the General Election of 1983, the Alliance obtained 25 per cent of the vote but only 4 per cent of the seats. Small parties like the Scottish National Party, whose support is concentrated in a particular part of the country, are more likely to win seats.

It is this lack of correlation between votes and seats which has given a strong impetus to the call for a different electoral system which would allow voters to express preferences between candidates so that if their first-choice candidate is not elected or has received sufficient votes to be elected, his second-preference votes can help to elect that candidate. Thus these votes are not completely wasted and a candidate may be elected because more voters have put him as their second choice. This system of voting can be used for one MP, i.e. in single-member constituencies (the alternative vote), or for several MPs, i.e. in multi-member constituencies (the single transferable vote). These systems give more chance to a third party such as the Alliance to win seats, because its candidates can be elected by being the voters' second choice. If this system were adopted in this country it would be very unlikely that either of the two main parties would win an overall majority of seats (i.e. more seats than all other parties combined) and this would have a profound effect on who would form the government.

CHOICE OF PRIME MINISTER

This brings us to the choice of Prime Minister who heads the government. In law it is the Queen who appoints the Prime Minister; in practice she must appoint the leader of the party which has won the majority of seats in the House of Commons. This forms the crucial link between the government and Parliament. All the main parties now elect their leaders so that the problems which arose in 1963 in finding a successor to Harold Macmillan as Conservative Prime Minister cannot recur. The Labour leader is now chosen by an electorate consisting of Labour MPs (30 per cent), the constituency Labour parties (30 per cent) and the trade unions (40 per cent), the Conservative leader by Conservative MPs, whilst the Liberal and SDP parties give a vote to each member of the party. If a party wins an overall majority of seats the choice of Prime Minister is clear but even under the present electoral system this did not happen in 1974, and if proportional representation were to be adopted it would become the exception rather than the norm. Where no party obtains a clear majority there are no legal rules, only conventional rules based on past precedents, which may not give a definitive answer because the situation is not identical and the rules are flexible. This flexibility would be lost if the rules were embodied in a written constitution. Ultimately the decision lies with the Queen and her advisers, though politicians will, if at all possible, settle the problem among themselves. What is the problem?

If the Prime Minister, who remains in office during the General Election, loses his overall majority he may try, as Mr Heath did in 1974, to form a coalition with another party in order to obtain such a majority. If he fails he should resign, as Mr Heath did, whether or not his party has won more seats than any other party (as Mr

Heath's did not in 1974). For the only alternative to resignation would be to ask the Queen to dissolve Parliament again and hold another election; and for this there is no precedent. The leader of the party with the next highest number of seats should, therefore, be asked to form a government. Unless he forms a coalition and obtains an overall majority he will be in a minority and risk defeat in the House of Commons. If this happens very soon, at the end of the debate on the Queen's speech, the problem arises whether he is entitled to ask the Queen to dissolve Parliament or whether she could refuse his request and ask the leader of the third party to try to form a government. In 1974 the minority Labour government was not defeated in this way and the Prime Minister did not ask for a dissolution until eight months had elapsed after the previous General Election. Whichever action the Queen took would involve her in controversy. To refuse the Prime Minister a dissolution would be unprecedented in modern times. To grant one so soon after the previous election would not only be undesirable but might lay her open to charges of partiality if she had already refused one to the outgoing Prime Minister. The only way out of this dilemma is for the parties to reach agreement among themselves either by forming a coalition or, if this is not possible, to allow a minority government a breathing space in which to govern, as happened in 1974.

PRIME MINISTER'S POWERS

Once appointed, is the Prime Minister an elective dictator with the powers of a medieval monarch, as Mr Benn has argued, or is he the *primus inter pares* (first among equals) in accordance with the classic system of Cabinet government?

Appointment and dismissal of ministers

The first and perhaps foremost power is that of appointing and dismissing ministers. In law, appointments are made by the Queen; by convention the power is exercised on the advice of the Prime Minister. The most important constitutional constraint, which again has grown up through convention, is that ministers must be or become members of either the House of Commons or the House of Lords. The holders of the most important offices (including the Prime Ministership itself) normally sit in the Commons, though there have been some notable recent exceptions such as Lord Carrington (Minister of Defence and Foreign Secretary) and Lord Young (Employment Secretary). The most important officeholders and other ministers of the Prime Minister's choosing are appointed members of the Cabinet which normally has between twenty and twenty-five members. This is the body which Bagehot (1867: 68) called 'a *hyphen* which joins, a *buckle* which fastens, the legislative part of the State to the executive part of the State'.

There are, of course, political constraints on the Prime Minister in appointing ministers. Senior members of the governing party, e.g. those who sat on the opposition front bench, will have a prior claim to be considered. But the situation would be transformed if, as Mr Benn (1980) has suggested, the Cabinet were elected by the MPs of the party in power in the same way as Labour MPs elect their Shadow Cabinet. The power of the Prime Minister would be cur-tailed even more drastically by his suggestion for annual elections, for this would take away the power of dismissal, which is the most potent instrument for moulding the Cabinet to the Prime Minister's will. The limits on this power are personal and political. Some Prime Ministers are more ruthless than others. The political constraints involve balancing the risks of opposition from the ex-minister on the back benches with those from keeping him within the Cabinet. Mr Benn was never dismissed from the Labour Cabinet, while Mrs Thatcher has steadily eliminated her opponents from her govern-ment. Mr Macmillan dismissed seven Cabinet ministers at one time in 1962. The political repercussions of such actions may not be immediately apparent. The penalty may not be paid until the next election in lost popularity. Before then it may lead to more oppo-sition from the government back benches. Though there is provi-sion now for both a Labour and Conservative Prime Minister to be challenged annually as Leader of the Party, it is in practice most unlikely for this to happen, because of the damage this would inflict on the party. Chamberlain was forced to resign in 1940 as Prime Minister because of criticism from within his party as well as by the opposition as voiced in the famous Norway debate (HC vol. 360, col. 1073, 7 May 1940). But in peace time it is in practice almost impossible for a Prime Minister with a majority of seats to be forced to resign by his party except on grounds of ill health.

Relationship between Prime Minister and Cabinet

The relationship between the Prime Minister and his Cabinet is also very much a matter of personalities, both his and theirs. The proponents of Prime Ministerial power point to the power to control the agenda of Cabinet meetings, the use of Cabinet committees appointed by the Prime Minister or informal groups of ministers instead of the full Cabinet for decision-making, the power derived from presiding over the Cabinet and summing up its discussions, and the close relationship with the Secretary to the Cabinet who is also the Head of the Civil Service. Each Prime Minister uses these powers differently and since Cabinet proceedings are held in secret we have to rely on the conflicting accounts of the participants after the event and unattributable leaks at the time. After thirty years Cabinet documents are made public (Public Records Acts 1958 and 1967). Exceptionally Cabinet documents may be made available to a committee of inquiry as happened in the case of the Franks review of the Falkland Islands (Cmnd 8787, 1983). Even more exceptionally, Cabinet secrets may be openly bandied about in the press and the House of Commons as happened in the controversy over the rescue of the Westland Helicopter Company. From these sources it is becoming increasingly clear that the Cabinet is no longer the strategic decision-making body which is implied in the phrase 'Cabinet government'. Not only is the agenda pre-empted by routine business and one-off cases which could not be resolved elsewhere but some very important issues have not been discussed there. These include Britain's atom bomb under Attlee, the Suez intervention by Eden, devaluation of the pound by Wilson, and, under Mrs Thatcher, the Falklands issue prior to the Argentine invasion, the banning of trade unions at GCHQ, the granting of consent to the USA to use its British bases for the bombing of Libya, and the rescue of the Westland Helicopter Company. It was the Prime Minister's refusal to allow this last issue to be discussed in Cabinet that led Mr Heseltine, the Defence Secretary, to charge Mrs Thatcher with responsibility for 'the breakdown of constitutional government' (*Observer*, 12 January 1986). The former Prime Minister, Mr Callaghan, thought this was overegging the pudding and put the blame squarely on the Cabinet. It was up to them to decide what they would put up with. 'If they behave like mice they must expect to be chased' (HC Deb., vol. 89, col. 1115, 15 January 1986). The ultimate weapon that a member of the Cabinet can use if he does not approve of what is being done in or outside the Cabinet is to resign, as Mr Heseltine did, but the weapon may turn out to be a boomerang.

COLLECTIVE RESPONSIBILITY

When a minister resigns because of disagreement with the Prime Minister and his colleagues he is observing the convention of collective responsibility. According to this rule of the constitution, each member of the government must support the government's decisions inside Parliament and outside. The corollary of this rule is Cabinet secrecy. The public unanimity would be exposed as a sham if the private disagreements were immediately revealed, or they would not be expressed if the participants knew in advance that they would be revealed publicly later. These considerations become weaker with the lapse of time. Though the thirty-year rule marks the legal termination of secrecy, fifteen years has been accepted as a conventional guideline for disclosure by ministers of confidential Cabinet discussions (Cmnd 6386, 1976). This followed the unsuccessful attempt to stop the publication of the sensational Crossman *Diaries* which revealed the inner workings of Mr Wilson's first government ten years later when Labour was again in power (*AG v. Jonathan Cape Ltd*, 1976). Both the unanimity rule and the secrecy rule have been more honoured in the breach than the observance. The rationale of the convention is to strengthen the government in whom public confidence is undermined by the exposure of open disagreements. But there have been occasions when open disagreement has been the only mechanism to prevent the government splitting apart and the convention has been deliberately set aside by an agreement to differ. This happened for the first time in 1932 in the case of a coalition government but it did not prevent the dissenting ministers resigning shortly afterwards. Mr Wilson followed this precedent in 1975, allowing open disagreement between members of the government over the government's recommendation to remain in the EEC, during the referendum campaign (HC Deb., vol. 889, col. 351, Written Answers, 7 April 1975). He did not extend this freedom to parliamentary proceedings and dismissed Mr Heffer for breaking this rule. Mr Callaghan set aside the convention in 1977 when allowing a free vote on a government Bill providing for direct elections to the European Assembly but did not extend this freedom to speaking against the Bill. When asked about this decision he made the revealing remark, 'I certainly think that the doctrine should apply, except in cases where I announce that it does not' (HC Deb., vol. 933, col. 552, 16 June 1977). Is the unanimity and secrecy convention a rule the Prime Minister can use or not to strengthen his position? The waiver of the rule can be seen in this light but it can also be regarded as a desperate remedy to prevent the government from disintegrating.

Unattributable leaks relating to Cabinet discussions are another safety-valve to preserve the facade of unanimity while at the same time allowing the hidden disagreements to surface without the source being revealed. These leaks may come from the Prime Minister as well as from dissenting ministers. Again Mr Callaghan spoke memorably: 'You know the difference between leaking and briefing. Briefing is what I do and leaking is what you do' (Cmnd 5104, vol. 4, p. 187, 1972).

Leaking still pays lip service to the rule, open disagreement between ministers breaks it. No Prime Minister can welcome this; it is a sign of weakness, not strength. To assert his authority, the Prime Minister must try to silence the minister or dismiss him. It was Mrs Thatcher's ultimatum to Mr Heseltine to observe collective responsibility in the Westland Helicopters affair that precipitated his walk-out from the Cabinet after retorting that he would accept collective responsibility where there had been collective decision-making. This correlation has not existed since the classic days of Cabinet government described by Bagehot. The unanimity rule has long been extended beyond members of the Cabinet and, as we have seen, the Cabinet is no longer the sole decision-making body. The acceleration of this trend under Mrs Thatcher was the basic constitutional issue raised by Mr Heseltine.

The other aspect of collective responsibility, namely responsibility to the House of Commons, is the fulcrum on which our parliamentary democracy turns. The House of Commons holds the power of life and death over the government but equally the Prime Minister can destroy Parliament by asking for a dissolution. The government can govern only so long as it does not lose the support of the House of Commons. If it does, today, in contrast to the earlier part of the nineteenth century, this would inevitably lead to a General Election. Again, in contrast to the earlier part of the nineteenth century, we have a rigid party system with strict discipline and loyalty. A government which holds a majority in the House of Commons can only be defeated as a result of a revolt by its own backbenchers, who know that a successful revolt will place their own seats in jeopardy at the ensuing General Election. It is not, therefore, surprising that the only two governments to be defeated on a vote of confidence this century have been minority governments, both Labour governments in 1924 and 1979. If the Leader of the Opposition puts down a motion of no confidence the government must by convention provide time for its early debate. The government may also itself seek a vote of confidence or deliberately make an issue one of confidence in order to put the maximum pressure on its supporters, though it is at the same time putting its life in their hands. It can also use a vote of confidence on an issue to reverse a previous defeat on the issue or alternatively it can accept the defeat. In the past a defeat on a major issue was regarded as a matter of confidence but governments no longer treat them as such. This development has enabled governments, in particular minority governments, to survive longer but it has also enabled backbenchers, especially rebel government backbenchers, to score victories against the government.

The convention of collective responsibility, the linchpin of our democracy, has thus contracted considerably in scope. It is now analogous to the ultimate deterrent whose fall-out is as lethal to those who use it as to those against whom it is used. The parallel convention of the individual responsibility of ministers has also undergone fundamental change.

INDIVIDUAL RESPONSIBILITY

The responsibility of individual ministers to the House of Commons can ultimately be enforced by the same mechanism as the collective responsibility of the government, namely by a vote of no confidence or censure. Though such a vote is not strictly one of confidence in the government, such a motion put down by the opposition will make the government side close ranks, and party discipline and loyalty will make the result a foregone conclusion. Individual responsibility is, therefore, brought about by other means. One must distinguish the responsibility of a minister for a matter of policy, for his personal behaviour and for the mistakes of his Department, though these do not form watertight categories.

Individual responsibility of ministers for policy matters merges into collective responsibility, for if the government disassociates itself from the policy of one of its members it is asserting collective responsibility in the same way as when a minister resigns because of policy disagreements with his colleagues. The resignation of Sir Samuel Hoare as Foreign Secretary in 1935, when the government repudiated the Hoare-Laval pact ceding Abyssinia to Italy because of the public outcry, can be seen as an example of such a resignation. However, the government had to admit to an error of judgement in first accepting the proposals, an error for which they did not offer to resign. Hoare was thus made a scapegoat for what was in effect a collective decision. Lord Carrington's resignation after the Argentine invasion of the Falkland Islands can be characterized in a similar way, for the policy prior to that invasion was that of the government and the resignation was made deliberately to conduct the lightning away from the government. Individual responsibility is here acting as a substitute for collective responsibility.

There is a similar blurring between individual and collective responsibility where the personal behaviour of a minister is under attack. The resignation of such a minister depends very much on the attitude of his colleagues and particularly that of the Prime Minister, though they are of course subject to outside pressures. Where the misconduct of the minister is not very serious, the Prime Minister can refuse to accept his resignation and thus condone his conduct, as happened recently in the case of Mr Robert Dunn, a junior

Education Minister whose entry in *Who's Who* was misleading about his academic qualifications (*Guardian*, 9 May 1986). In effect he is being protected with the shield of collective responsibility. If the public is sufficiently outraged this may not be politically possible. This happened in the case of Mr Cecil Parkinson. Mrs Thatcher stood by him at first when the affair with his secretary became public after the General Election of 1983. But after her revelations to *The Times* the public outcry and pressure within the party forced Mrs Thatcher to accept his resignation. Similarly Mr Macmillan could not have shielded Mr Profumo, who lied to the House over his affair with Christine Keeler. That a Prime Minister cannot always save a minister whose personal conduct is under attack is well illustrated by Mr Brittan's resignation over his leaking of a confidential letter from the Solicitor-General to Mr Heseltine during the Westland Helicopters affair. As Mr Brittan wrote in his resignation letter, he could no longer command the full confidence of his colleagues once he had been identified as the leaker, even though, as Mrs Thatcher wrote in her reply (in words similar to those in her reply to Lord Carrington's resignation), she had tried her utmost to dissuade him from resigning (*Guardian*, 25 January 1986). These cases demonstrate the limits on Prime Ministerial power to save a minister, limits imposed by public opinion, by colleagues collectively and by the sense of honour of individual ministers.

It has been argued that similar considerations apply to the responsibility of a minister for mistakes made by his Department (Finer, 1956: 394). The resignation of Sir Thomas Dugdale in 1954 over mismanagement in his Department of the sale of a piece of land called Crichel Down is the classic and arguably the last illustration of a minister resigning for the faults of his civil servants of which he neither knew nor could have known. A former colleague, Lord Boyle (1980: 10), has claimed that Dugdale resigned because he stood by his decision rather than for the misconduct of his officials. His resignation was certainly not required according to the rules laid down by the Home Secretary in the debate on the matter (HC Deb., vol. 530, col. 1285, 20 July 1954). The civil servants were not carrying out his orders or acting in accordance with his policy. He did not have to defend the misconduct of his officials but he had to render an account to Parliament of his stewardship. Mr Prior rejected the Crichel Down case as a precedent when he was under pressure to resign after the mass break-out from the Maze Prison in Northern Ireland. He argued that it was not his policy that was to blame but failures in carrying out security procedures at the prison (HC Deb., vol. 53, col. 1041, 9 February 1984). This distinction between policy and administration was strongly criticized by MPs but it is difficult not to agree with the verdict of his junior minister that the constitutional convention requiring ministerial resignation in such a case 'had not existed in politics in this country for many years' (ibid., col. 1108).

CIVIL SERVICE

The convention of ministerial responsibility regulates not only the relationship between ministers and the House of Commons but conversely that between ministers and civil servants. Civil servants are not elected but appointed officials who are responsible to their ministers. They advise ministers on the formulation of policy and carry it out. As a corollary they are normally protected by anonymity and are politically neutral, serving each government in turn. This relationship has been subjected to great strains recently and its hallmarks are being challenged and eroded by both ministers and civil servants.

If civil servants are found blameworthy by an inquiry whose report is published, as happened in the Crichel Down and Maze Prison cases, their names inevitably become public. These are, however, exceptional cases. Normally the report of an internal departmental inquiry would not be published. There was no intention originally to publish the findings of the inquiry by the Secretary to the Cabinet into the leaking of the Solicitor-General's letter in the Westland affair. It was a leak from this inquiry and the naming of the civil servant who leaked the letter which led to the Prime Minister's statement that the leak had been authorized by Mr Brittan and his subsequent resignation (HC Deb., vol. 90, col. 449, 23 January 1986). The constitutional significance of the affair for the Civil Service lies in the identification of the civil servants in the

Department concerned with the leaking and those in the Prime Minister's office who were consulted and the alleged misunderstanding between them. Though Mr Brittan accepted responsibility for the actions of his officials, the officials in the Prime Minister's office have been publicly identified without being shielded by ministerial responsibility. This has been said to be turning ministerial responsibility on its head (*Guardian*, 11 March 1986). However, in accordance with the strict convention of ministerial responsibility, these civil servants have not been allowed to give evidence to the House of Commons committee investigating the affair because it is a matter for ministers to decide which officials appear before these committees (HC 169, 1985–6, Q. 1064, Evidence to Defence Committee) and Mrs Thatcher has added that for private secretaries and personal staff to give evidence would have major implications for the conduct of government (HC Deb., vol. 90, col. 1091, 30 January 1986). The Secretary to the Cabinet, the Head of the Civil Service, who did give evidence to the committee, argued that the officials should not be subjected to a second inquisition (HC 519, 1985–6, para. 226). The committee was not impressed by this argument but endorsed the view that the officials concerned might well have welcomed the opportunity to explain their actions in public, which would have enabled Parliament to consider who was responsible for any mistakes and who ought to have been held accountable (ibid., para. 238; see Chapter 6, below).

According to the rules drawn up by the Secretary to the Cabinet himself, restating the relationship between ministers and civil servants, it is for ministers to decide what information should be made available and they are ultimately responsible (HC Deb., vol. 68, col. 130, Written Answers, 26 February 1985). As civil servants were not being asked to act unlawfully in leaking the confidential letter to the press (as the minister can authorize the publication of otherwise confidential information) they would seem to have been following the guidance to the letter. Nevertheless, the House of Commons committee did not think that the minister's authority was sufficient in the circumstances (HC 519, 1985–6, para. 173).

The problem facing the civil servants in the Westland affair was analogous to that of Mr Ponting, a civil servant whose acquittal for leaking confidential information contrary to the Official Secrets Act

1911 gave rise to the guidelines of the Secretary to the Cabinet. Mr Ponting, an official in the Ministry of Defence, leaked information to an MP because he felt that ministers were withholding information from a committee of the House of Commons. Ponting argued that he owed a higher duty to the House of Commons than to his minister. This argument would make civil servants accountable to the House of Commons rather than to ministers. The guidelines firmly reject this proposition. The only concession they make to a conflict between the minister's instructions and the civil servant's conscience is where the action is unlawful or where it is contrary to a deeply held personal conviction on a fundamental issue of conscience, but even there, if the issue cannot be resolved through his superiors, he is expected in the last resort to resign. To solve this dilemma suggestions have been made for a code of conduct which would allow civil servants to take the issue to an outside body. This has been rejected by the government but they have accepted that in such cases a civil servant should be able to appeal to the Head of the Civil Service (Cmnd 9841, 1986, para. 19). Lord Scarman (1985) has argued for legal safeguards as part of a written constitution.

These cases are exceptional but they do raise in an extreme form the fundamental principle that civil servants must be politically neutral and not sit in judgement on a government's policies. Constitutionally it is not their function to curb what has been called 'the worst excesses' of a radical government whether of the left or right (HC 535-1, 1976-7, Chapter XIII – Expenditure Committee Report on the Civil Service). They were accused by some Labour politicians as a result of their experiences in government as having arrogated to themselves the role of governing the country. These politicians detailed the tactics of delay and obstruction as well as the civil servants' built-in advantages in obstructing the policies of the government and implementing their own departmental policies. These antics have been parodied in the *Yes, Minister* programme which, like all good caricatures, contains more than a grain of truth. Since Mrs Thatcher came to power the boot has been on the other foot. Complaints have come predominantly from the Civil Service that they are being politicized. This, it is alleged, is happening in several ways (see HC 92, 1985–6, part V – Treasury and Civil Service Committee Report on Civil Servants and Ministers).

First, it is being done through appointments. The Prime Minister is involved in all appointments of permanent secretaries, the Civil Service head of a Department. She is credited with asking whether a potential appointee is 'one of us'. This does not mean a party man but one who is in tune with the style and ethos of the government. This has profound significance for the next government of a different political colour who will have to work with men, many of whom have been appointed by Mrs Thatcher.

This problem is not limited to the top echelons of the Civil Service but permeates down the hierarchy. If men whose faces fit get promoted to the top, the rest will follow suit and become 'Yes' men. They will give the advice ministers want to hear to gain promotion rather than objective advice which may be unpopular. In the Prime Minister's introductory statement to the Cabinet Secretary's guidelines to civil servants she expressly refutes this charge, saying, 'No competent minister wants his civil servants to tailor their advice to what they think the minister wants to hear.' Nevertheless, in the present climate of government the temptation is great.

Perhaps the most reprehensible form of politicization is misusing civil servants to perform party political functions. The line between governmental and political functions may be fine but there is a distinction. The use of a civil servant to leak the Solicitor-General's letter in the Westland affair can be said to be abusing the function of a civil servant, and Mrs Thatcher says she deeply regretted the method for bringing the letter into the public domain (HC Deb., vol. 90, col. 653, 27 January 1986). Again the position of the Prime Minister's press secretary who briefs newspaper correspondents on an unattributable basis, i.e. without allowing the source to be quoted, in a controversial and partisan manner is more suitable for a party politician than a civil servant.

The logical corollary of these developments is a political Civil Service where the higher echelons change with the government, as happens in the USA. There is some feeling that the time has come for such a development here, but it has grave drawbacks for practical reasons such as lack of continuity and expertise as well as depriving ministers of a source of independent advice. Political advisers whom ministers bring into the Department from outside the Civil Service are a compromise solution which could be expanded further (HC 92,

1985–6, part V; see Chapter 6, below). It has even been suggested that backbench MPs should be included in such teams of advisers (HC 535–1, 1976–7, p. lxxxi) but this would have important constitutional implications for the role of Parliament vis-à-vis the government, which will now be examined.

2

Parliament

THE HOUSE OF COMMONS

The House of Commons, which is the elected Chamber (the House of Lords will be discussed later), has a dual function: its role is both to sustain the government and to criticize it. This dichotomy runs through much of the work of the House of Commons and is the key to understanding the paradox that often Parliament is used as a synonym for the government because it acts as a rubber stamp; but it is also used in antithesis to the government, i.e. as a control mechanism. It would not be a solution to this conflict to say that the majority of the House fulfil one function and the opposition another, for the role of critic is performed by both sides of the House. Nor would it be correct to say that the role varies according to which task the House is performing, i.e. whether it is legislating or asking questions, for its critical and sustaining roles cut across these functions. It is when voting rather than expressing opinions that this dual role becomes most sharply focused, for MPs then have to make a clear decision as to whether to support the government or not. A vote of no confidence is, as we have seen, the ultimate weapon for defeating a government but almost certainly today at the cost of a dissolution of Parliament. Defeats on other issues illustrate the controlling function better because, unlike the bee's sting, they can be used more than once. Even these are likely to be rare and it is the daily give and take of debate and questioning which bring pressure to bear on the government, particularly under the constraints of time and coupled with the threat of possible defeat, that wring concessions and compromises from the government, thus still making the House of Commons (and to a lesser extent the House of Lords) an important check on the elective dictatorship of the government.

That this check is by no means as powerful as it was in the last century is due to the growth of the party system which controls, first, who gets elected as an MP and then how he votes once he is an MP. We have seen how difficult it is under our electoral system to be elected unless one belongs to one of the two main parties; it is virtually impossible if one belongs to no party, though there have been some isolated exceptions. Once elected, the MP is the representative of his constituency which, as Edmund Burke made clear in his famous address to his Bristol constituents in 1774, does not constrain him to vote in accordance with their interests, i.e. he is not their delegate. In fact it is a breach of privilege of the House punishable as contempt for an MP's freedom of action to be fettered by an outside body. This has given rise to problems where MPs are sponsored by a trade union who contribute to his expenses or where they have other outside paid interests such as directorships or consultancies. Such interests are not banned, because the House would then become a body of professional politicians, but the House has resolved that they must be disclosed in debate and other proceedings and declared in a register of interests open to public inspection (HC Deb., vol. 874, col. 391, 22 May 1974). These rules do not have the force of law but the House can use its own sanctions of suspension or expulsion to enforce them. These measures are designed to prevent conflict between an MP's private interests and his duty to represent the public interest. In reality, however, the biggest constraint on an MP's freedom of action comes from the party system.

Whipping

The mechanism for exerting pressure on an MP to toe the party line is the system of whipping. The Chief Whip and his assistant whips are members of the government whose task it is to ensure that MPs on the government side vote in accordance with the party whip which is a summons to vote graded according to importance, the three-line whip being the most peremptory. The opposition operates a similar system for its members. It has been argued recently by an MP that the whip is no more than a summons to attend the House but leaves the MP free to vote according to his judgement (HC Deb., vol. 95, col. 595, 14 April 1986). This may be true in theory but bears little relation to reality. A Tory MP has graphically described the pressures to which rebel or potentially rebellious MPs are subjected and the threats and cajolements which are brought to bear before a vote such as that on the pay review for senior civil servants, military and judges where there is a serious danger of a government defeat (*Guardian*, 2 August 1985). The ultimate deterrent of a General Election was hinted at, though probably not seriously. There are many lesser pressures which can be brought to bear, varying from not being allowed to go on a trip abroad with a parliamentary delegation, to not being considered for a ministerial post and being reported to the Constituency Chairman. These pressure points epitomize the bondage of an MP to his party which reinforces the party loyalty which an MP naturally feels. They also distinguish today's MPs from their nineteenth-century forebears, who were not dependent on their seats for their livelihood, as many MPs are today.

Nevertheless, the pressure does not always work and some MPs are known as regular rebels. The crunch comes when the rebellion is large enough to inflict defeat on the government. The increase in such defeats in the 1970s (sixty-five defeats on the floor of the House of Commons between 1972 and 1979) has been noted (Norton, 1982: 112). Most of these were, however, inflicted on the minority Labour government between 1974 and 1979 and are therefore not typical for a majority government but more a foretaste of things to come under a hung Parliament. However, a large majority can also be dangerous for a government, as Mr Pym remarked during the 1983 General Election, a warning which probably contributed to the loss of his Cabinet post. Mrs Thatcher's government, with a majority of 146, has suffered defeats, most notably on the Shops Bill providing for Sunday opening (HC Deb., vol. 95, col. 694, 14 April 1986). The government tried to forestall defeat by offering a free vote on the later stages of the Bill. A free vote is traditionally used for non-party political issues of conscience (e.g. the abolition of capital punishment) but it can also be used to prevent defeat, as happened in the case of the Bill providing for direct elections to the European Assembly. In that case the free vote extended, as we saw, to members of the government (Chapter 1). Some free votes are less free than others. In the debate on the Water (Fluoridation) Bill members of the government were whipped (ibid., col. 689), and this also happened in the important debate on the procedure for Bills which will be considered shortly. Normally whipping applies not only on the floor of the House but when a Bill is considered in detail in committee. Defeats on amendments to the Bill are more frequent here because the majority of the government is smaller in proportion to the size of the committee. Such defeats can be reversed when the Bill returns to the floor of the House to be further amended. However, in the case of the Civil Aviation Bill in 1985 government rebels, who objected to the expansion of Stansted Airport, managed to get the committee stage halted altogether (Standing Committee F, 12 February 1985) and the Bill was abandoned, but this did not ultimately prevent the limited expansion of Stansted Airport.

It is arguable, therefore, that MPs hold the control of an elective dictatorship in their own hands. They have the vote and if they used it more frequently in accordance with their judgement rather than the party whip, the power of the government would be markedly curtailed. Undoubtedly MPs could exercise more independence and such a development would be accelerated in a hung Parliament, i.e. where no party had an overall majority. But it would be simplistic to underestimate the pressures of party loyalty and the party whips. The most potent antidote to the latter would be a system of voting in secret in the House of Commons instead of by walking through the lobbies. The potency of this system was shown in Israel, where it is used for the election of the President by MPs, when a Labour President was elected by a majority of MPs of the other parties in 1983. It is also revealing that the election of the party leader by Conservative MPs is by secret ballot. However valid in principle the arguments in favour of secret voting may be – and it has been made obligatory by this government for officers of trade unions (Trade Union Act 1984) – it is utopian to imagine that any government would concede the power this would confer on its backbenchers to defeat its policies with impunity except on a vote of confidence, where there would be the threat of dissolution. Such votes of confidence would probably then become more frequent.

The role of the opposition

Since such a utopian solution to the elective dictatorship is unlikely, the main burden of opposition to the government inevitably lies with the opposition. This has been institutionalized in a number of ways. Most significantly perhaps, the Leader of the Opposition is paid a salary as are a few other opposition officeholders (Ministerial and Other Salaries Act 1975), and in addition money is made available from public funds to opposition parties for their parliamentary work (HC Deb., vol. 888, col. 1869, 20 March 1975) – at present a maximum annually of nearly half a million pounds. Many would like to go further in strengthening advice for the opposition, to the extent of seconding civil servants to their staff (Wass, 1983). The rights of the opposition are enshrined in the procedure of the House of Commons. As we have seen, a motion of no confidence tabled by the opposition must be debated as soon as possible. At Prime Minister's question time and when business for the coming week is announced by the Leader of the House, the Leader of the Opposition is given priority over other MPs. In debate speakers alternate between government and opposition, and membership of committees is proportionate to the membership of the House. One of the problems encountered by the SDP-Liberal Alliance is that House of Commons procedure is adapted for the two-party system and does not easily accommodate a third party. This has led to a series of protests by the Alliance to procure recognition, most notably to obtain a share of those days expressly set aside for the opposition on which they may choose the subject for debate.

Supply procedure

These 'Opposition days' have an interesting history which is symptomatic of the relationship between the government and the House of Commons. Their origin lies in the days set aside for the discussion of public expenditure in the form of the annual estimates which, when embodied in the annual Appropriation Acts, legalize central government expenditure for that year. Originally there was no limit on the number of days set aside for discussion of the estimates. It was Balfour in 1896 who bargained a fixed number of days in return for a fixed date by which all the estimates had to be put to the vote. On these Supply days, as they came to be called, the opposition was given the right to choose the subject for debate. Increasingly, these days have been used by the opposition to discuss government policy rather than the details of government expenditure. There was rarely even a vote taken on whether an estimate should be granted to the government, and the Appropriation Acts, which legalized the expenditure, were passed purely formally without discussion except for the occasional protest at the farce that parliamentary control of expenditure had become. In 1982 the pretence of discussing expenditure on Supply days was dropped and they became called Opposition days. In addition three days were set aside for the discussion of expenditure, to be called Estimate days (HC Deb., vol. 28, col. 118, 19 July 1982). These days have been used for the discussion of reports of committees of the House which have been critical of particular areas of government expenditure. The debate takes place on a motion to approve a particular estimate which is then formally passed at the end of the debate. No amendment to reduce an estimate has so far been put to the vote. The House of Commons has thus abdicated its function of discussing the details of government expenditure or even challenging them to a vote, preferring instead to use the allotted time to discuss issues of government policy selected by the opposition or one of its committees. This is partly the result of the intractability of the subject-matter and the inclination of politicians to discuss politics rather than economy of expenditure, but it also shows the dangers of a time-limit by which the House has to give its approval to government business, as it deprives the opposition of its strongest weapon which is time.

Legislative procedure

This has been the main topic of debate in relation to the procedure for approving legislation other than that authorizing government expenditure. The House has not abdicated its function to scrutinize the details of legislation including the annual Finance Act which authorizes taxation. Detailed discussion normally takes place not in the House as a whole but in standing committees, where the Bill is discussed clause by clause and line by line. It is here that concessions can be wrung from the government by applying pressure both from outside the House and within. A good illustration is the Police and Criminal Evidence Bill on which there were 105 sittings in committee (it had to be reintroduced after the General Election of 1983) and which ended as a very different Bill from the original one. Pressures were exerted by bodies like the Law Society, the BMA, the police and other professions outside the House, whilst the opposition and government backbenchers kept up a steady stream of amendments in the House. In many cases these were then adopted by the government in a modified form. The pressure is most potent when government backbenchers join forces with the opposition to make defeat possible. Even where this does not happen, the opposition have the weapon of time, because the government needs to get its legislative programme passed at the latest by the end of the parliamentary session (normally October) as it lapses otherwise. The government has a counter-weapon, the guillotine, a procedure which fixes a timetable for a Bill and automatically cuts off debate at the stated time. This is the equivalent procedure for Bills which applies automatically in the case of the estimates.

In theory this procedure could be used for all Bills, as it only needs a vote at the end of a three-hour debate in the House to impose it. In practice it has only been used in a handful of Bills, though the number has been growing recently. It is used for highly party-politically controversial Bills which the opposition would otherwise delay indefinitely or for a very long time. In such cases the committee stage becomes a time-wasting filibuster by the opposition until the guillotine is imposed. To prevent this charade of all-night sittings with endless repetitive speeches by the opposition whilst government backbenchers write letters or sleep, it was recommended by the Procedure Committee of the House of Commons that all Bills which were likely in the opinion of a committee of senior MPs to take more than a certain number of hours in a standing committee should be subject to a timetable fixed by the senior MPs (HC 49, 1984–5). It was this recommendation which was rejected in the vote mentioned earlier where backbenchers but not members of the government were allowed a free vote and there arose the unusual spectacle of the government uniting with the opposition to defeat its own backbenchers in order to preserve the rights of the opposition (HC

Deb., vol. 92, col. 1083 seq., 27 February 1986). One could argue that this debate epitomized our form of representative democracy, which is encapsulated in this passage from the speech of the Leader of the House, Mr Biffen: 'All governments are tomorrow's possible opposition, and I think that my Right Hon. and Hon. Friends, in their moments of supreme confidence, should consider, at least theoretically, how these proposals would bear upon the opposition. The Westminster political process is oblique and wide-ranging. It is like a seamless robe, which includes government legislation, and much else. At present, the opposition have open-ended opportunities for time and debate on legislation. If these are automatically extinguished, the opposition will be deprived of a pressure point which is often used to secure accommodation from the government, not merely on legislation, but on other points in the political process' (ibid., col. 1088). The Opposition Leader of the House, Mr Shore, congratulated Mr Biffen on his far-sighted and generous speech.

Select committees

The model of parliamentary government which is implicit in the extract from Mr Biffen's speech is one of adversarial politics, where the government proposes and the opposition opposes and obtains modifications of the government's proposals by internal and external pressures. There is a totally different political model, namely the consensus model, where the aim is to reach agreement across the political divide by compromise and bargaining. The end result may be similar, as compromise may be achieved by either means, but the method used will be completely different. Whether our adversarial politics is the result of our two-party system or not, the parliamentary procedures and the physical shape of the chamber of the House of Commons are geared to this system. Countries with multi-party politics have horseshoe-shaped chambers which symbolize the gradation of the political spectrum rather than its sharp division. If and when the two-party system breaks down in Britain and if proportional representation is adopted, coalition governments will have to be formed, which will involve moving towards the consensus model of politics. Even under our present adversarial system the alternative consensus model is followed in one area of House of Commons procedure, namely that of select committees. These committees, unlike the standing committees which consider legislation, do not debate but take evidence from witnesses by questions and answers and then normally make a report based on that evidence to the House as a whole. They have no powers except to make recommendations. They are constructed on the consensus model which is epitomized in their horseshoe-shaped seating arrangements.

The oldest select committee is the Public Accounts Committee which is the only mechanism by which the House of Commons examines the economy, efficiency and effectiveness of government expenditure. It has the assistance of expert auditors under the Comptroller and Auditor General whose reports to the committee form the basis of their examination of witnesses from government departments. Its chairman is by convention a senior opposition MP, to signify its impartiality and non-partisan nature. The same applies to the committee which scrutinizes delegated legislation (orders made by ministers under the authority of an Act of Parliament). The most important development of select committees came in 1979 when fourteen committees were set up to scrutinize the work of each government department by examining its expenditure, administration and policy. The then Leader of the House said that they could constitute the most important parliamentary reform of the century (HC Deb., vol. 969, col. 35, 25 June 1979) which could alter the balance of power between the government and Parliament. Has this happened?

To emphasize the independence of the new committees the nomination of their members was entrusted not to the party whips but to another committee of the House (the Committee of Selection) who have evolved their own conventions, such as the exclusion of all frontbench spokesmen, which is intended to lessen partisanship. They employ expert advisers, usually on a part-time basis, and have power to order the attendance of witnesses and the production of documents. The limits of this power can be seen in the Westland Helicopter inquiry. As we have seen, the government refused to allow the civil servants involved in the leaking of the Solicitor-General's letter to give evidence to the Defence Committee inquiring into the affair. The committee could have enforced attendance only through an order of the House of Commons where the government has a majority. It has reported the circumstances to the House in its report on the Westland affair (HC 519, 1985–6, para. 231). No committee has yet taken a disagreement with the government about the production of evidence to the floor of the House. Either the government has produced the evidence, and much evidence has been made available to committees which would not otherwise have seen the light of day (including confidential minutes in the Westland affair), or the committee has climbed down and accepted the refusal. Though the government has promised to make time available for a debate if there was widespread concern in the House at the refusal to make evidence available to a committee, such a debate and the subsequent vote would put to the test whether MPs put loyalty to their committees above that to their party. This would be a litmus test of whether the balance of power between the government and Parliament had been changed by the committees.

The inquiries conducted by the Defence and Trade and Industry Committees into the Westland affair illustrate one of the novel features of these committees. They can and do investigate instantaneously matters of current concern in a way that the House of Commons cannot do, namely by calling all those concerned, including ministers, to be questioned in depth and then reporting their findings to the House. The Education Committee was even able to settle an industrial dispute threatening the Proms by giving both sides an opportunity to state their case (HC 722, 1979–80). This function of the committees to gather information from interested parties and the government and make it available to the House and the public has advanced the cause of open government to the extent that the government uses their existence as an alibi for a Freedom of Information Act.

This function, however, does not fundamentally change the balance of power between government and Parliament. To do this committees must carry weight with the government and Parliament. It is very difficult to evaluate the committees' impact on the government, as they are one among many influences brought to bear. Their recommendations are most likely to bear fruit where the government is already thinking along the same lines, e.g. the Home Affairs Committee's report on the law relating to public order (HC 756,

1979–80). But they can also give an added impetus to reforms, such as the same committee's report recommending abolition of the 'Sus' law, which probably would not have happened without the strong pressure of the committee (HC 744, 1979–80). If the committees can report before the government has crystallized its policy, they are more likely to have an impact on government policy than by criticizing it *ex post facto,* though the policy-making process is a continuing one and the mere existence of the committees will make the government sensitive to their anticipated reaction, knowing that they will be called there to answer for their actions.

The impact of a committee's report is greater when it is unanimous than if it splits along party lines. There have been spectacular examples of such splits, notably the Foreign Affairs Committee's report on the events surrounding the sinking of the Argentine cruiser *Belgrano* (HC 11, 1984–5). However, the vast majority of reports have been unanimous and where there have been votes on parts of the report these have often cut across party lines. The striving for consensus could be said to be the hallmark of the committees. It is achieved partly by the choice of subjects for investigation. It was almost inevitable that an issue as emotive as the sinking of the *Belgrano* would give rise to fundamental disagreement. This has not, however, prevented the committees from dealing with highly controversial party political issues, such as the banning of trade unions at GCHQ, and reaching consensus on them (HC 238, 1983–4). In other cases a party split has been avoided by not making recommendations or by openly registering disagreement in the report. But in many cases subjects would not be chosen for investigation where a party split is a foregone conclusion. The achieving of consensus is made more difficult if the draft report by the chairman is prematurely leaked so that pressures can be brought to bear on members of the committee to toe the party line rather than make the compromises necessary to reach agreement, which is more likely to be reached behind closed doors. The decision of the House to treat such leaks seriously as breaches of parliamentary privilege, and to punish them accordingly, failed at the first attempt to apply it to a *Times* journalist who published a leaked report from the Environment Committee, because the person who leaked the report to him could not be found (HC Deb., vol. 98, col. 293, 20 May 1986).

The consensus model which select committees follow is a source of weakness as well as strength. They exist as an oasis in an adversary system. This system limits both their functions and effectiveness. If they were given powers other than the power to make recommendations, the party whips would bring to bear the same pressures on members as they do in the House itself and the committees would split along party lines. The most fundamental weakness is the difficulty in transferring the consensus of the committee to the House itself. One of the novel features of the new committees is the extent to which they have tried to dovetail their reports with the work of the House. Though their reports are not often debated as such, in many more cases they are specially prepared in time for a debate on the subject. This has been particularly true of the Treasury Committee's reports on public expenditure. But increasingly committees try to report on matters of public concern in time for a debate in the House. The new Estimate days are, as we have seen, used for debates on reports of the committees, though this still falls far short of a systematic examination of expenditure by the committees before approval by the House. Some committees have also made reports whilst a Bill is passing through Parliament in order to influence the legislative process. It is when such issues on which the committees have reported come to a vote in the House that the loyalty of members of the committees is put to the test. With some notable exceptions, e.g. in the debate on the 'Sus' report (HC Deb., vol. 985, col. 1763, 5 June 1980), members have voted with their party rather than their select committee and the consensus of the committee has not been transferred to the House itself. Thus the committees have not altered the balance of power between the government and Parliament because they have not broken through the party political barrier. The crux of the matter was summed up by Mr Cunningham, a rebellious right-wing Labour MP who later defected to the SDP, when he said, 'In this place honourable Members often look for procedural prescriptions to ailments which are not procedural in nature but personal' (HC Deb., vol. 2, col. 1258, 10 April 1981). In other words the balance of power cannot be changed by improving procedures by select committees but by MPs using their votes.

THE HOUSE OF LORDS

The unelected part of Parliament, the House of Lords, is an anachronism. It consists of over a thousand peers, the majority of whom (over seven hundred and fifty) have inherited their titles and most of whom do not attend. The average daily attendance is about three hundred. Since the Life Peerages Act 1958 it has been possible to create life peers who, like the hereditary peers, are created by the Queen on the advice of the Prime Minister, who in some cases consults the opposition parties. There are now over three hundred life peers and they have transformed the party composition of the House of Lords. Though the peers taking the Conservative whip still form by far the largest group in the House of Lords, they no longer have an absolute majority over all the other peers, a considerable number of whom (about two hundred and fifty) sit on the cross-benches, which signifies their non-allegiance to any party. This group particularly includes former civil servants, the law lords who are created life peers under an Act of 1876 and those peers who have held high judicial office, e.g. Lord Denning. This change in party composition of the House of Lords through the creation of life peers and the non-attendance of most hereditary peers has profoundly affected the functioning of the House of Lords (Shell, 1985).

The House of Lords ceased to be the dominant part of Parliament as a result of the reform of the franchise in the nineteenth century, which made the House of Commons pre-eminent as the democratic chamber. But the House of Lords still had co-equal power over legislation, as all Bills had to be passed through the House of Lords as well as the House of Commons. Conventions developed about ultimately giving way to the elected House and there was always in the background the threat that the Prime Minister could ask the monarch to create sufficient peers in order to pass the legislation. It was this threat which enabled the great Reform Act 1832 to be passed. The threat was never put into practice (after 1712) but it played an important role in the constitutional crisis of 1909–11 when the House of Lords rejected the Liberal government's budget proposals. This led to a General Election which was won by the Liberal government. The King promised to create sufficient peers to force the House of Lords to assent to the curtailment of their powers provided that this met with the approval of the electorate. After a second General Election, which enabled the government to remain in power, the Parliament Act 1911 was passed which abolished the veto of the House of Lords for most Bills but not one which extended the life of Parliament beyond five years. Instead, they were able to delay Bills for up to two years which was cut down to one year in 1949. Again this power is more of a threat than a reality. The 1911 Act was only used three times to pass an Act, one of which was the Parliament Act 1949. No law has yet been passed without the consent of the House of Lords under the 1949 Act, though the House of Lords used its delaying power for a year on a Trade Union Bill in 1975 and only allowed it to pass when the approval of the Lords was no longer necessary for it to become law. It is not, therefore, the use of the delaying power which is important, but its existence in the background still enables the House of Lords to wield considerable power over the content of government legislation. The exercise of this power operates under different constraints depending on whether a Labour or Conservative government is in office.

The problem of the House of Lords whichever government is in power is that it is unelected. This problem is accentuated when a Labour government is in office because of the in-built Conservative majority in the House of Lords, even though this is no longer absolute. Therefore, if the House of Lords uses its delaying power against a Labour government it will be accused of acting party-politically and obstructing the will of the people as expressed through the elected government. In retaliation the Lords will be threatened with abolition or at best reform. To cope with this dilemma conventions were evolved after the Second World War when a Labour government was elected for the first time with a large majority. The House of Lords would not use its delaying power for a Bill for which the government had a mandate, i.e. a proposal which was contained in the manifesto of the party which won the election. They would use this power only for a matter of great constitutional and national importance, to enable the government to think again and to allow public opinion to be mobilized. This convention was broken in 1976 when the House of Lords refused to pass the Aircraft and Shipbuilding Industries Bill which provided for the nationalization of those industries and which had been promised in the

Labour Party manifesto. Lord Carrington, who was then the Leader of the Opposition in the House of Lords, justified the action by reference to the Parliament Act itself. He said that it was for a situation such as this that the Act was devised, that unless the House of Lords had some power it would be useless and that the government was a minority one (HL Deb., vol. 377, col. 1678, 22 November 1976). In the end the Bill became law without the ship-repairing industry being included, in accordance with the wishes of the House of Lords. Apart from delaying the Trade Union Bill and emasculating the Aircraft and Shipbuilding Bill, the House of Lords defeated the Labour government 355 times between 1974 and 1979 (Shell, 1985). Such defeats may be irreversible when the Bill returns to the House of Commons if the government is in a minority or only has a small majority or needs to pass the Bill by a certain date. It was the experience of the Labour government between 1974 and 1979 which made the Labour Party Conference in 1977 vote for abolition of the House of Lords, though this was not included in the 1979 manifesto by Mr Callaghan; it was however contained in the 1983 manifesto.

The position of the House of Lords when a Conservative government is in office is very different. If it uses its power to defeat the government it cannot be accused of acting party-politically because of the Conservative majority there, though it can be accused of acting undemocratically if it votes against a manifesto commitment. On the other hand a Conservative government cannot in practice use either the Parliament Act to override the House of Lords or the threat of abolition if they defy the government. In practice a Conservative government may have to accept defeats by the House of Lords which a Labour government would be able to reverse. Until recently, however, such defeats have been rare. Mr Heath's government was defeated only 26 times but Mrs Thatcher's government was defeated 45 times in the 1979–83 Parliament (Shell, 1985), and more than 55 times in the sessions since then. These figures are impressive but they cannot be compared with those inflicted on the Labour government of 1974–9. The most important defeat came over the Bill to abolish elections for the GLC and the other metropolitan counties preparatory to the abolition of those local authorities. By convention the House of Lords does not vote against the second reading (the first debate on the principle of a Bill) where there is a manifesto commitment to which the Bill gives effect. However, at the next stage a fundamental amendment was carried to postpone implementation of the Act, because it would have allowed interim bodies with a different party political composition to take over the work of the existing councils before they had been legally abolished (HL Deb., vol. 453, col. 1069, 28 June 1984). This was considered unconstitutional by speakers in the House of Lords. The paradox lay in the unelected House defeating the elected House for acting undemocratically. The House of Lords was in fact performing the precise constitutional function which is the main justification for its existence. They were on a matter of great constitutional importance using their powers to make the government think again, a power which they alone could in these circumstances perform since the government had a majority of 146 in the House of Commons. With supreme irony the House of Lords, with Lord Hailsham, as Lord Chancellor, presiding on the Woolsack, was curbing the elective dictatorship to the delight of Ken Livingstone, the Chairman of the GLC, whose party is in favour of abolition of the Lords.

The paradox of the House of Lords is that as an anachronistic and unelected body its constitutional justification is to act as a check on the elected House. The Parliament Act 1911 recognizes this explicitly in exempting a Bill to extend the life of Parliament from its provisions. Even its worst enemies, like Mr Benn, recognize that if the House of Lords were abolished this constitutional gap would have to be filled. Other mechanisms would also have to be found for revising Bills that have passed through the Commons. The proposals for reform of the composition of the House of Lords are all aimed at removing the anomaly of an unelected House, where one party has an in-built majority, acting as a revising chamber for legislation and ultimately as a constitutional safeguard. No solution has so far been found acceptable. The proposals of the Labour government in 1968 (Cmnd 3799) came nearest to being implemented but the Bill embodying them was torpedoed in the House of Commons through delaying tactics by an unlikely alliance of abolitionists, led by Michael Foot, and traditionalists, who wanted to keep the status quo, led by Enoch Powell. The proposals would have eliminated the anachronistic element by depriving most hereditary peers of the power to vote whilst allowing them to continue to sit in the House and speak. They would also have abolished the permanent Conservative majority through the creation by the government of the day of sufficient peers to give them a majority over all other parties but not over the whole House including the cross-benchers, who take no party whip. The cross-benchers would, therefore, have held the balance of power, though they rarely act as a cohesive force. The proposals would have increased the patronage in the gift of the Prime Minister and still have given power (though slightly reduced) to delay legislation to an unelected House. An elected House of Lords, which has been suggested by Lord Hailsham (1976) as well as others, would inevitably be a rival to the House of Commons and was rejected in 1968 on those grounds. Because of the difficulty of finding an acceptable solution for the reform of the composition of the House of Lords, the present anachronistic House is likely to continue for the foreseeable future. Thus the ultimate paradox of the House of Lords is that its strength lies in its archaic weakness.

3

Allocation and Methods of Decision-making

All decision-making powers of public authorities derive from Parliament with the exception of those derived from the prerogative. These are the residual powers of the Crown which derive from the common law. They include such important powers as declaring war, making peace treaties, dispatching the armed forces, e.g. sending the Task Force to the Falklands and even requisitioning merchant ships, including the *QE 2*, during the Falklands conflict (Requisitioning of Ships Order 1982). Because power derives from the prerogative the government does not need the authority of Parliament for the exercise of these powers, though in practice Parliament will be informed in such important cases, as happened in the famous debate on Saturday, 3 April 1982 (HC Deb., vol. 21, col. 633) before the Task Force was dispatched to the Falklands. Similarly, the instruction given by the Prime Minister prohibiting civil servants at the Government Communications Headquarters (GCHQ) from being members of a trade union, another illustration of a prerogative power, was announced to Parliament but only after it had been given, presumably for reasons of national security (HC Deb., vol. 52, col. 917, 25 January 1984).

Lack of time constrains Parliament to delegate power to make rules to other bodies, particularly to ministers. The interpretation and application of Acts of Parliament and delegated legislation to individual cases is also entrusted by Parliament to a variety of bodies such as tribunals, ministers, public corporations and local authorities.

DELEGATED LEGISLATION

Parliament can make only a limited number of decisions in the form of legislation. Acts of Parliament should lay down the principles but their detailed implementation has to be delegated to ministers. The

Act will give power to a minister to make regulations, called statutory instruments, for this purpose, i.e. rules drafted in his Department which the Act may provide shall be laid before Parliament either for approval or for annulment. In the former case the government has to provide time to debate the instruments for at least one and a half hours, though in some important cases more time has been allowed for debate. In the case of annulment MPs, normally from the opposition, have to put down a prayer and debates are held after 10 p.m. and are cut off at 11.30 p.m., when the vote takes place, which, if the government has a majority, will normally be a foregone conclusion. Of the approximately two thousand statutory instruments which are made every year the vast majority are not subject to parliamentary approval and only a small number of prayers are debated late at night. There is thus little opportunity to debate statutory instruments on the floor of the House and no possibility of amending them unless a minister can be persuaded to withdraw the instrument and bring it back in a different form. It is now possible for statutory instruments to be debated in a standing committee but they have to return to the House to be approved or annulled there.

The lack of parliamentary scrutiny is inherent in the use of statutory instruments, as they are intended to save parliamentary time. So long as they deal with the nuts and bolts of legislation this is acceptable. There is, however, a growing tendency to use statutory instruments for matters of policy and principle which should be embodied in the Act itself. This is a dangerous development, as it gives wide powers to the government which are not subject to detailed scrutiny by Parliament. It has been suggested that there should be a mechanism for identifying such instruments and allowing them to be debated at greater length and possibly providing an opportunity for amendment (HC 257i, 1985–6).

Social security legislation offends particularly in this respect. Many important matters are left to be dealt with in regulations, often because ministers have not made up their minds on the issue at the time of the Bill, or regulations may be used for purposes which were unforeseen at that time. A good example of the latter are the board-and-lodgings regulations which fixed maximum amounts and time-limits for young people to claim benefit. The regulations were intended to discourage the young unemployed looking for work from staying in seaside resorts. These regulations were declared illegal by the courts because the limits were not contained in the regulations themselves, but the minister was given power in the regulations to lay down such limits, which he did in a separate booklet (*R v. Secretary of State for Social Services ex parte Cotton*, 1985). This could be altered without having to obtain parliamentary approval. After the judgement declaring the regulations unlawful, new regulations were eventually made which fixed the limits by referring to the booklet expressly and these new regulations were held to be valid by the court (*R v. Department of Health and Social Security ex parte Camden LBC,* 1986). Changes in the booklet would thus involve changes in the regulations. This case illustrates ministers circumventing even the minimum formality of statutory instruments by laying down rules in less formal documents which did not have to be laid before Parliament.

This development from formal to informal methods of laying down rules has grown at an enormous rate recently. Whilst at one end of the spectrum statutory instruments are being used for provisions which should be contained in Acts of Parliament, at the other end statutory instruments are being replaced by codes of practice, codes of conduct, guidelines, circulars and a miscellany of rules which have been given the title of 'quasi-legislation'. Unlike statutory instruments, this material has varying degrees of legal force. Its legal effect will depend on the Act under which it is made. The Highway Code is probably the first illustration of this development. Breach of the code is not a criminal offence but it can be taken into account in any criminal or civil proceedings (Transport Act 1982, section 60). This provision has been used in an increasing number of areas including health and safety at work, industrial relations, race relations, animal welfare and control of pollution. The main reason for using codes with limited legal effect in preference to legal regulations was a preference for the voluntary approach. In these situations it was thought that persuasion would be more effective than compulsion and codes would be more advisory and persuasive than legal regulation. They also have the practical advantage of not having to be couched in precise legal language and they can also be more flexible. However, their flexibility will depend very much on the procedural safeguards which regulate their making and approval. Here there are a plethora of different provisions in the parent Acts but certain standard control mechanisms recur in many statutes. There is often provision for consultation with affected interests, parliamentary approval or the opportunity for annulment and publication. The difficulty of locating this material, because publication takes such diverse forms, has been one of the main criticisms of these mechanisms for laying down rules from the beginning of this development.

Quasi-legislation is used to regulate the conduct not only of private individuals but also of public authorities. The codes of practice made under the Police and Criminal Evidence Act 1984 may be regarded as a prototype. These lay down the way in which the police should exercise their functions under the Act in much more detail than the Act itself. Breach of the codes makes the police liable to disciplinary proceedings but does not render them liable to criminal or civil proceedings, though it must be taken into account in such proceedings where relevant (section 67). Similar provisions are now contained in statutes concerned with local government and provide for codes directed to local authorities. The novelty lies in embodying in Acts of Parliament provisions for such codes of guidance to local authorities. Until recently such guidance, usually contained in circulars from a government department to local authorities, was provided without any statutory provisions. This is still the position in most cases. The circulars are often a mixture of explanation and advice and they have been used in some cases as a substitute for legislation because the government preferred persuasion to legal regulation of local authorities. Thus circulars were used by the Labour government in 1965 to implement its policy for comprehensive education, and legislation was only used as a last resort to bring a few recalcitrant authorities to heel in 1976.

Quasi-legislation can be abused when it is used to by-pass Parliament by putting politically controversial provisions in a code of practice instead of an Act of Parliament. This happened with the code on picketing, made under the Employment Act 1980, which limited the number of pickets to six, a figure which was not included in the Act, but has become law by the back door, because the code has to be taken into account by the courts. Where there is consensus

50

on a code it can be more effective than law in ensuring compliance, as well as having practical advantages, but the procedures for the making, publication and parliamentary scrutiny of codes need to be systematized.

INTERPRETATION AND APPLICATION OF LEGISLATION AND DELEGATED LEGISLATION

Tribunals

Rules, whether laid down in an Act or in regulations made under an Act, have to be interpreted and applied to individual cases. Interpretation of statutes and statutory instruments is a matter for the courts but Acts of Parliament may entrust this function to other bodies, though, as we shall see, these will themselves be subject to the supervision of the courts. In an increasing number of areas tribunals have been preferred to courts as decision-making bodies. There are over two thousand tribunals covering such diverse areas as social security, immigration, employment, rents, taxation, rates and the national health service. The reasons for preferring tribunals to courts are both practical and ideological.

Tribunals do not consist of lawyers, though increasingly the chairman is a lawyer appointed by the Lord Chancellor. The other members may be representatives of interest groups, e.g. employers or employees in the case of industrial tribunals, or they may have a particular expertise, e.g. doctors in the case of mental health tribunals. When some of the tribunals were first set up after 1945 it was made explicit by the government that the courts were not trusted to decide disputes in certain areas of social policy such as national insurance, rent and the national health service. Later criticism centred on the members of tribunals being drawn from a narrow social spectrum and being unfamiliar with the problems of the people appearing before them, particularly in the case of supplementary benefit appeal tribunals. It has also been alleged that in certain cases tribunals have been used to give the appearance of impartiality to the implementation of controversial policies. This allegation has been made particularly against supplementary benefit appeal tribunals and immigration tribunals (Harlow and Rawlings, 1984, p. 75 seq.). The policies are embodied in the Acts and regulations or rules made under them, the tribunals can only interpret and apply them. If ministers do not approve of the interpretation in a particular case, it can always be reversed by changing the law. Ministers cannot interfere directly in individual cases but they have been known not to publicize unfavourable decisions so as to limit their impact, or to settle test cases in order to prevent an unfavourable decision. Tribunals were firmly categorized as part of the machinery for adjudication rather than administration by the Franks Committee which was asked to investigate the constitution and working of tribunals in 1955 (Cmnd 218). To achieve impartiality, which was one of its aims for tribunals, it recommended that members should be neither appointed nor dismissed by ministers. This was only partly implemented so that chairmen are usually appointed by the Lord Chancellor or from a panel of members appointed by him, and all members can normally be removed only by him. As most members hold office only for a limited period, this latter safeguard is not very significant.

The practical advantages of tribunals are procedural. In general they are cheaper, quicker and more informal than courts, though the variations between tribunals are as great as their differences from the courts. Some, like the Lands Tribunal, are indistinguishable from a court in all but name, whilst in a social security tribunal all the participants, including the members of the tribunal, may sit round a table. In between these extremes of formality, the members of an industrial tribunal may sit on a raised dais with the parties sitting at tables in front of them. Procedure varies accordingly from an almost informal conversation round the table to a full-scale hearing with the parties represented by lawyers and evidence on oath. Legal aid is not available for representation before most tribunals and many applicants, therefore, appear in person or may not appear at all in the case of social security tribunals. Some see the remedy for this in making legal aid or other representation more widely available, so that the parties are more evenly matched. Alternatively, it is possible to see the members of tribunals playing a more active role in the proceedings, as many do in practice, by asking questions and bringing out the salient issues. There is also evidence that applicants prefer to play a more active role in the proceedings rather than listening passively to their lawyer present their case (Bell, 1975, p. 16). If tribunals are too closely modelled on courts they lose the procedural advantages which were the main justification for their creation. On the other hand, they must be seen to be fair and independent from the government department concerned if they are to be trusted by the citizen.

Ministers

Ministers entrust to courts, tribunals or any other independent body those individual decisions which they do not wish to take themselves, though they usually reserve the power to lay down the policies to be applied by such bodies. The rationale behind such allocation is very varied and by no means consistent either between governments of different party political complexions or even between those of the same political colour. Thus the Labour opposition opposed giving wide discretionary powers to the Restrictive Practices Court to determine whether restrictive trade agreements were against the public interest. On the other hand a subsequent Labour government entrusted wide discretionary powers to immigration tribunals when determining immigration appeals, which was opposed by the then Conservative opposition. In contrast, governments of both parties have refused to entrust decisions about the provision of grants to assist industry to a court or tribunal, even where detailed criteria were laid down by statute, because they wished to reserve questions of interpretation to themselves. Again, governments of both parties may agree to give wide discretionary powers to an independent body so as to eliminate political considerations, e.g. the allocation of contracts by the Independent Broadcasting Authority. When governments want to take into account their own policy in reaching a decision and do not want to entrust its interpretation to another body, they will reserve the decisions to themselves, though in practice only the most controversial cases will be decided by ministers personally. The rest will be decided by civil servants in the Department, the level at which the decision is made depending on its importance.

Where decisions are made by government departments in the name of the minister the procedure may be completely informal.

This is the position with regard to grants to assist industry. These are negotiated between the applicant and officials in the Department who interpret the statutory provisions and internal guidelines which supplement them. A firm which may be disadvantaged by the granting of assistance to a rival concern has no opportunity to object. Governments have rejected all attempts by MPs to formalize these procedures by making the Department give reasons for its decision, though applicants are given guidance about the criteria that the Department uses. Governments have insisted on retaining the maximum flexibility for these potentially politically sensitive decisions, refusing to be bound by any appeal mechanism or outside advisory body.

PUBLIC INQUIRIES

In marked contrast to this informal decision-making process for decisions which can involve the public expenditure of millions of pounds for projects such as Concorde or the Rolls-Royce RB211 engine, is the elaborate public inquiry procedure which is obligatory for a vast number of decisions varying from the appeal against a refusal of planning permission to the building of roads, airports and nuclear power stations. It is revealing that the same basic procedure is prescribed for such widely disparate decisions, whose only common feature is that they involve interference with private land and that their origin lies in the private Act of Parliament which at one time had to be passed before these rights could be taken away compulsorily. The procedure for passing such Acts, which were used for the building of the railways and canals, is very cumbersome and expensive, involving an elaborate judicial-type hearing before a small committee in each House. As we shall see, the building of the Channel Tunnel is being authorized by a similar procedure. This is, however, an exceptional case, and in general, because of the cumbersomeness of private Acts, power to hold the inquiries was delegated to government departments. They appoint an inspector who conducts the inquiry and reports to the minister; he, or in most cases his officials, then makes the decision, usually without any parliamentary involvement. This is, therefore, another illustration, like delegated legislation, of ministers having taken over a function from Parliament.

The use of the public inquiry for such vastly different types of decision has led to its transformation from a procedure for safe-guarding private property rights to an instrument for public participation in major issues of national policy. The public inquiry procedure still performs its original function of protecting land-owners in the run-of-the-mill appeal by an applicant against refusal of planning permission by a local authority. In most of these cases the power to make the decision is now vested in the inspector, which in practice means that they are made by a different type of official, as few decisions reach the minister himself. In most cases the applicant now opts for an informal written procedure but he has the statutory right to a full oral hearing at a public inquiry. At such an inquiry the main protagonists are no longer just the local authority who refused permission and the applicant for such permission, but third parties, i.e. neighbours and those concerned with the wider environment who, though they have no legal rights, are allowed to state their views to the inquiry and whose representations may be taken into account. This has turned many such inquiries into contests between private landowners rather than resolving conflicts between the private and public interest, though the public interest is only an amalgam of private interests. A neighbourhood is merely a collection of neighbours. As has been said elsewhere, one man's property is another man's environment (Ganz, 1974: 55).

The judicialization of inquiries received a strong impetus from the Franks Committee (Cmnd 218, 1957) which was asked to investi-gate the procedure of inquiries as well as tribunals. It made many recommendations, which were mostly implemented, to make the procedure more like a court hearing than an administrative proce-dure designed to inform the minister. Reasons now have to be given for decisions and the inspector's report has to be published, and the minister cannot disagree with his findings except on matters of policy without giving the parties further opportunities to make rep-resentations or reopening the inquiry. As a result, inquiries have become more court-like with parties represented by lawyers, adopting courtroom techniques of cross-examination before an inspector whose judicial appearance Franks wanted enhanced by putting his appointment into the hands of the Lord Chancellor. This has not been implemented, except many years later in the case of motorway inquiries, but the natural corollary of these developments has been to turn the inspector into the judge who makes the decision in the case of most planning appeals which are not politically controversial. The controversial cases can always be called-in for decision by the minister and it is in these major inquiries into projects such as the building of a third London airport, or a new type of nuclear power station at Sizewell or, to a lesser extent, the building of motorways that most problems have been encountered in adapting the highly judicialized public inquiry procedure as a prelude to important political decisions.

By widening the terms of reference of the inquiry to investigate the need for the project, in addition to its siting at a particular place, and by adding expert assessors to assist the inspector, who can commission his own research, the inquiry has been broadened into an investigation of major political and economic issues such as the desirability of nuclear power or airports policy. This examination takes place within the straitjacket of a court-like procedure with the major participants represented by high-powered lawyers. The inspector's report and recommendations are made to the minister and the ultimate decision in such important cases may well be made at Cabinet level. The inspector's recommendations, reached after years of investigation, may be overturned for purely political reasons, as happened to the recommendations of the Roskill Inquiry into the siting of the third London airport in 1971. Parliament has as a rule no legal role to play in these decisions, which it has conferred on ministers, but recently it has insisted on debating the issues before decisions are made. This has involved difficult contortions so as not to fall foul of the legal provisions relating to the handling of the inspector's report by the minister. All these difficulties epitomize the problem of reaching a political decision through a judicial procedure. A two-stage procedure has been recommended whereby the policy issues about the need for the project are investigated by a more inquisitorial type of procedure, preferably without lawyers, and only if approval is given for the project would there be a public inquiry into where it should be sited (Outer Circle Policy Unit, 1979). Unfortunately the multi-stage Roskill Inquiry, which lasted for two and a half years, has made governments wary of adopting such procedures.

In stark contrast to these public inquiry procedures for major projects is the building of the Channel Tunnel, which will be authorized by an Act of Parliament, with a committee stage like a private Act, where objectors will be heard. This will be the substitute for the public inquiry which has been steadfastly refused by the government as being too time-consuming. The categories of persons entitled to object and the grounds on which they may do so are matters on which the decision lies with the parliamentary committees, but they will not hear argument on the principle of having the Channel Tunnel. In a sense the Channel Tunnel is a return to the classic days of the nineteenth century when Parliament decided such issues. The volume of criticism that this procedure has aroused is perhaps an indication of how far we have moved from a representative to a participatory democracy, where individual citizens and pressure groups expect to be consulted.

CONSULTATION AND OPEN GOVERNMENT

The consultation of affected interest groups before decisions are made by the government is well established in certain areas but is by no means universal. Acts of Parliament are normally preceded by intensive consultation with those affected and Bills are often preceded by consultation papers, sometimes called Green Papers, followed by White Papers setting out the government's proposals on which further consultation takes place before the Bill is drafted. Both types of document may also be debated in Parliament. Similar procedures may be used for delegated legislation. Some town planning regulations have been preceded by consultation papers and the Highway Code has been through a Green Paper stage. Consultation on statutory instruments which may go through many drafts is now the norm, though this is rarely provided for by statute. In the case of statutory codes of practice there is frequently a duty to consult affected interests embodied in the statute. Even non-statutory circulars have been subjected to intensive consultation, such as the Department of Environment circular dealing with green belts round built-up areas. There have also been startling examples of the lack of consultation, such as the instruction by the Prime Minister prohibiting employees at the secret Government Communications Headquarters from being members of trade unions, which the courts would have held to be unlawful but for the considerations of national security involved (*Council of Civil Service Unions v. Minister for the Civil Service*, 1984). It has even been held by the Court of Appeal that a non-statutory circular on immigration by the Home Secretary could not be changed without giving an applicant in receipt of the circular an opportunity to make representations (*R v. Home Secretary ex parte Asif Khan*, 1984). But it is doubtful whether this case can be applied generally to changes of policy by which individuals are deleteriously affected.

Consultation may be institutionalized by making it obligatory to consult an advisory body, as is the case with social security regulations. It is also now becoming more common for the departmental select committees to consider regulations, codes of practice and even circulars before they are debated in the House of Commons or reach their final form. Such committees also examine policy statements from the government which may be contained in White Papers and preceded by Green Papers. Both Green Papers and White Papers may invite further comments from the public, though this is more usual with the former than the latter. Draft policy statements may also be used for this purpose. There is enormous variation in the extent to which the policy-making process by the government is open to public debate. The review of the supplementary benefits scheme by a team of officials in the Department of Health and Social Security in 1978 (Social Assistance) was not only published but members of the team answered questions at meetings throughout the country. This was a rather exceptional exercise in open government. Though there was a general directive by the Head of the Civil Service in 1978 to publish factual background material to policy studies unless ministers decided otherwise (HC Deb., vol. 942, col. 691, Written Answers, 26 January 1978), a later Head of the Civil Service stated that the reasons for deciding against publication might often be nothing more weighty than political embarrassment (Wass, 1983). The degree of political embarrassment which can be caused by exposing the policy-making process to public view was nowhere better illustrated than during the Westland affair when Cabinet meetings and confidential departmental meetings were openly discussed in Parliament and the media. Similar revelations followed the acquittal of Mr Ponting under section 2 of the Official Secrets Act 1911 for leaking information about the sinking of the *Belgrano*. One can see these spectacular leaks as symptoms of a system of closed government which should be opened up legally by a Freedom of Information Act which would give a right to the citizen to see government documents which did not fall within certain exceptions such as defence, security, international relations and probably also Cabinet papers and confidential advice from officials. Repeal of section 2 of the Official Secrets Act 1911 would lift criminal sanctions from all but a narrow range of sensitive information, though it would still leave officials open to disciplinary sanctions for leaking confidential information. Whether government becomes more open by law or by further concessions from governments or by more leaks or not at all remains to be seen. Without information, participation in decision-making is impossible and democracy becomes devalued.

Quangos and nationalized industries

Where governments want to take decisions out of the political arena but do not want to entrust them to the courts or tribunals, they can allocate them to a public body set up for this purpose. These bodies can be loosely described as quasi non-governmental organizations (quangos). They can be used for very different purposes and set up by governments of opposite political persuasions. Some exist with all-party agreement, others are subject to acute political controversy. At some times they are very much in fashion, at other times severely under attack, and these fluctuations cut across party lines. The Labour government after 1945 set up public corporations to run the nationalized industries or non-commercial services such as the New Town Development Corporations. Mr Heath's Conservative government in 1970 followed the advice of the Fulton Committee on the Civil Service (Cmnd 3638, 1968) to hive off activities from the Civil Service for reasons of managerial efficiency. Mrs Thatcher has waged war on quangos as symbols of patronage, bureaucracy and public expenditure but this has not prevented her from creating new ones where she thought it necessary, such as the urban development corporation for London's Docklands and the boards which have taken over some of the functions of the GLC and Metropolitan

County Councils which were abolished by the Local Government Act 1985. Some bodies like the BBC, the Independent Broadcasting Authority, the Arts Council and the University Grants Committee have been generally recognized as useful buffers protecting the area in question from direct political interference. On the other hand, the National Enterprise Board and its predecessor, the Industrial Reorganization Corporation, set up by Labour governments to give assistance to industry, were each axed by the succeeding Conservative governments because they were not politically acceptable. Quangos are neither good nor bad, the basic question is to what extent it is desirable that decisions should be distanced from political considerations and be taken by experts applying commercial, artistic or professional criteria. The corollary of independence from political control is lack of democratic accountability, though there may exist other forms of public accountability.

This question has been most hotly debated in the case of the nationalized industries. When the majority of the nationalized industries were created after 1945, the model adopted was the arm's length approach whose architect was Herbert Morrison. The essence of this model is that ministers are responsible for policy but the boards of the industries are to be free from political interference on day-to-day matters of management. This blueprint was enshrined in the nationalization Acts by reserving to ministers powers to appoint and in certain situations dismiss the chairmen and members of the boards in charge of the running of the industries, the power to give general directions on matters affecting the national interest, the need for ministerial approval of certain programmes such as development or reorganization involving substantial capital expenditure, and the ability to request information at any time. Most importantly from a practical point of view, if an industry could not meet its financial obligation to break even, it was the government who had to provide the money. These provisions were intended to give ministers strategic powers of control but to leave the boards freedom to manage the industry within the framework set by the minister and in particular to fix the prices and wages within the industry. This model did not work according to plan. The nationalized industries were too important to be left alone, particularly in the area of prices and wages. If there was a major strike on the railways or in the mines, negotiations took place with union leaders who at one period were invited to No. 10 Downing Street to talks over beer and sandwiches. If there were elections in the offing, pressure was brought to prevent a price increase in a key industry. Mostly pressure was not exerted through a general direction having legal effect under the statute but by informal discussions between the chairman and the minister which were given the nickname of lunch-table directives. The minister would either have appointed the chairman or be in a position not to reappoint him, the term of office usually being for five years. Where the industry needed money, the minister would be in the most powerful position to twist the chairman's arm. Very few general directions were ever issued and it is doubtful whether they could have been legally given in many of the situations where pressure was brought to bear on specific issues. Labour governments used their powers to make particular industries perform social obligations which were financially uneconomic, e.g. build a power station which was not yet needed, to provide employment. Mr Heath's government used the nationalized industries as the spearhead of his incomes policy by making them keep prices down.

This political interference with the running of the industries blurred the responsibility for their management and efficiency and played havoc with their finances. It became accepted that an industry which was asked to perform unprofitable social obligations should be compensated by the government (Cmnd 3437, 1967), though the means and extent were often the subject of much controversy. In spite of this concession, it was generally recognized that the relationship between ministers and the nationalized industries was unsatisfactory. In 1976 an independent inquiry recommended a new approach (National Economic Development Office). Instead of the arm's length approach which it thought had broken down and which it rejected as inappropriate for industries so vital to the economy of the country, it recommended a new structure based on cooperation between ministers and industries in a new body (the Policy Council) to be inserted between the minister and the boards where mutually agreed policies would be hammered out. Concertation rather than separation between minister and industry was to be the key. The Labour government, significantly, rejected these recommendations as imposing an unnecessary additional layer between the minister and the board (Cmnd 7131, 1978). It also disputed that there could be a clear-cut distinction between strategic decisions to be taken by the Policy Council and managerial decisions to be taken by the board of the industry, but it eagerly embraced the committee's recommendation to give ministers a last-resort power to give specific and not just general directions, which it promised to use sparingly. This promise never had to be implemented because Mrs Thatcher's government which followed had a very different philosophy towards the nationalized industries.

In theory the Conservative government espoused a hands-off approach. The nationalized industries were to be treated like private industry and the aim was that they should all as soon as possible pay their way and not rely on government subsidies. This did not prevent the government bringing pressure to bear on the Chairman of British Steel to reprieve a steel plant in Scotland (Ravenscraig) for employment reasons (HC 212, 1982–3: Report of Industry and Trade Committee). There were also allegations of governmental interference during the miners' strike of 1984–5 in spite of the government's declared policy of neutrality. The overriding constraint imposed by the government was the financial limit within which each industry had to work. These limits determined how much an industry could borrow, or, if it was profitable like the gas and electricity industries, how much money it had to pay back to the government. These limits were fixed with reference to the government's monetary policy and they in turn determined the prices which the industry had to charge. Thus the government's economic policy determined the prices which the consumer had to pay rather than the financial state of the industry. Non-interference by the government was therefore practised more in theory than reality. The government also made proposals for legislation (1984) to give ministers greater legal powers over the nationalized industries which have been unanimously opposed by the industries.

The Conservative government's main solution to the problems arising from the relationship between the government and the nationalized industries is de-nationalization. The slogan is that the proper business of government is not the government of business. However, privatization has not eliminated the problem of governmental interference. The government still retains a stake in some industries, e.g. British Telecom where only just over 50 per cent of the shares were sold. Even where all the shares have been sold, the government may retain a special share to use in case of a foreign takeover or other emergency. The government has declared that it will treat these companies in the same way as a private sector company and will not use any shareholding it retains to interfere in the commercial decisions of the company except in the circumstances envisaged for the use of the special share. It does, however, retain the power to use its shareholding where this exists, as in British Telecom, and a subsequent government would *a fortiori* not be bound by this declaration. The revelation of the pressures brought to bear on British Aerospace, in which the government only retained a special share, to withdraw from the European consortium which made a bid to take over Westland Helicopters, and the arm-twisting to which the fully private firm of Westland itself (as supplier of helicopters to the armed services) was subjected by both camps in the government make a mockery of the policy of non-interference with industry which the government professes.

The relationship between ministers and the nationalized industries illustrates that governments of all political persuasions exercise substantial political control over these bodies (in some cases even after privatization) because they are of vital importance to the national economy. Similarly, governments exercise varying degrees of control over other quangos through the power of appointment of members, the power to give directions and guidance, approval and appeal procedures and above all financial constraints where the body is dependent on public funds. Ministerial control over such bodies is, therefore, much greater than over tribunals exercising judicial or quasi-judicial functions, though some quangos like the Civil Aviation Authority, which grants air transport licences, perform similar functions.

Local authorities

The relationship between the central government and local authorities is again a different one. Local authorities are the only public bodies apart from the House of Commons which are directly elected. Local councillors, therefore, represent and are accountable to their local electorate which gives them a legitimacy quite different from that of an appointed body and which can lead to direct conflict with central government, particularly one of a different political persuasion. However, in our constitution, whose linchpin is the sovereignty of Parliament, the central government with a majority in the House of Commons has the last word through being able to pass legislation. The increase in recent years of legislation to regulate the relationship between central and local government is indicative of its breakdown, as traditionally this has been based on consensus, consultation and cooperation rather than law.

Local authorities derive all their powers from Acts of Parliament in which the government of the day lays down its policy in respect of a particular subject-matter whether it be housing, education or town and country planning and delimits the functions which local authorities perform in that field. Local authorities in this country have no general powers to carry on activities outside their statutory powers, though they are entitled to spend a very small amount of their rate income for the benefit of the area or its inhabitants. Central government not only lays down the framework of powers and duties to be performed by local authorities but may impose detailed controls over their exercise. Local authority plans laying down their policy on a particular subject-matter may be made subject to ministerial approval, e.g. development plans under the Town and Country Planning Acts. Again these Acts provide a right of appeal to the minister against a refusal of planning permission by a local authority. Similar ministerial powers exist in many other areas of local government. Bye laws made by local authorities also need ministerial confirmation, and certain appointments need ministerial approval. In respect of some functions, e.g. police and education, ministers have powers of inspection, and legislation often confers on ministers reserve powers to act where the local authority has failed to perform one of its functions. Ministers may also in some cases have power to give directions to local authorities or provide guidance for the exercise of a function, e.g. the provision of social services. An increasing number of Acts make provision for such guidance to be issued, which was formerly and is still in many cases provided without specific authority, usually in the form of a circular. As we have seen, such circulars have often been used as a means of persuading local authorities to adopt certain policies in preference to enacting legislation making such policies obligatory. The increasing use of legislation to impose central government's policies on local authorities indicates the breakdown of consensus, and nowhere is this more marked than in the case of local government finance whose control enables central government to wield most power over local authorities and which has given rise to the greatest conflict.

Local authorities derive their finance from rates, central government grants, charges and fees, and in the case of capital expenditure mainly from loans and capital receipts. The main conflict between central and local government in recent years has arisen over the attempt, particularly by Mrs Thatcher's government, to control local government expenditure in furtherance of the government's economic policies. The previous Labour government had tried to curb local authorities' current expenditure by imposing strict limits to prevent the central government grant increasing in line with local expenditure and by reducing the total grant available to all authorities if they collectively overshot the totals of expenditure indicated by central government. The Conservative government changed the law in the Local Government, Planning and Land Act 1980 so as to enable the grant allocated to individual authorities to be tailored to reflect the extent to which they complied with the figure which the central government department determined to be the correct expenditure for each authority, so that increases in expenditure above a certain level attracted less grant. Even though this figure was not legally binding, it represented an inroad on the autonomy of local authorities to determine their own expenditure. A further inroad followed when the Local Government Finance Act 1982 allowed the minister to reduce the grant to which an authority would otherwise have been entitled, if it spent over a new set of targets which were superimposed on the existing limits. These penalties were intended further to deter overspenders who now included even some authorities who had spent within the government's original limits. Again these measures did not have the desired effect because local authorities could make good the shortfall of income from government grant by levying higher rates to finance their expenditure. This led the government in the Rates Act 1984 to take powers to impose rate-capping on local authorities which allowed the minister to fix the maximum rates of those authorities who spent above another set of limits laid down by the minister. Thus the power of a local authority to fix its own rates was for the first time interfered with by central government. This led to a rebellion of the affected local authorities, most of whom refused at first to set any rate at all. One by one the rebel authorities succumbed under the threat of their councillors being surcharged with the money lost. This is done by the court on the application of the district auditor who audits the accounts of local authorities. Surcharging may lead to disqualification from holding office and certain councillors eventually suffered this fate. There was no rebellion over rate-capping in the following year. Some of the overspending authorities, i.e. the GLC and some of the metropolitan counties, were among the authorities abolished in the Local Government Act 1985. The result of these developments is another step towards more centralized government.

The reverse trend towards decentralization suffered a severe setback when the Labour government's devolution proposals were not accepted in referenda in Scotland and Wales in 1979. Directly elected assemblies would have been set up in both countries, who would have performed some of the functions at present vested in the central government and quangos. There were no provisions for the devolution of functions in England to a regional tier of government. This could come about through a reform of the structure of local government. The Labour Party has proposed the abolition of all county councils leaving only a single tier of local authorities, district councils, throughout the country thus extending the present position in the seven large conurbations (London and the metropolitan areas) to the rest of the country. Above this tier there would be directly elected regional councils who would perform some of the functions at present vested in the central government and quangos as well as some of those vested in county councils. Decentralization may, therefore, come from below through a reorganization of local government and a clawing back of functions which have been lost to central government and quangos or by a restructuring of central government and devolving power to assemblies in the countries and regions of the United Kingdom. Either solution would diffuse power within the confines of a unitary state and leave the sovereignty of Parliament intact. Lord Hailsham's proposals (1976) for a federal structure where the powers of the assemblies in the countries and regions of the United Kingdom would be enshrined in an Act of Parliament, which could only be changed by a special procedure, envisages a written constitution for the United Kingdom which would involve a complete break with the past.

4

Control Mechanisms and Public Accountability

There are a number of mechanisms whereby those who exercise the functions discussed in the previous chapter can be supervised, monitored and held to account. The courts, though numerically they deal with only a small number of cases, are perhaps constitutionally the most significant because the subjection of public authorities to the ordinary courts is the cornerstone of the rule of law as formulated by Dicey in his *Law of the Constitution* (1885, Chapter IV).

COURTS

The courts cannot act as courts of appeal from any of the bodies examined in the previous chapter unless there are express statutory provisions to this effect. They do, however, possess the power to review the decisions of such bodies unless there are express statutory provisions excluding judicial control. Judicial review is more limited than appeal as it is not concerned with the merits of the decision but with its propriety, though in practice the distinction may be a fine one.

Judicial review

The proper remedy for reviewing the actions of public authorities is an application for judicial review, but where the applicant's private rights are infringed by a public body the private law remedies of declaration and injunction still apply (*O'Reilly v. Mackman*, 1983). There are important procedural differences between an application for judicial review and the other remedies, which provide safeguards for the public authority whose decision is being challenged. Leave has to be obtained from a judge for the application to proceed.

There are strict time-limits within which proceedings must be started and cases are heard by a judge drawn from specialists in administrative law. Evidence is presented in the form of written affidavits rather than orally through witnesses, a procedure which is not suitable for resolving disputed questions of fact, which will not normally be at issue in such proceedings. The applicant must have a sufficient interest in bringing the proceedings which means that he must be more than a mere busybody, but whether a taxpayer has such an interest has given rise to much controversy (*Inland Revenue Commissioners v. National Federation of Self-Employed*, 1982, and *R v. Her Majesty's Treasury ex parte Smedley*, 1985).

The grounds on which judicial review may be allowed have been categorized by Lord Diplock in his judgement in *Council of Civil Service Unions v. Minister for the Civil Service* (1984: *GCHQ* case) where judicial review was requested of the Prime Minister's instruction prohibiting staff employed in the Government Communications Headquarters to be members of a trade union. He classified the grounds for judicial review under three headings, namely, illegality, irrationality and procedural impropriety. The case decides that the same grounds of review are available whether the powers are derived from statute or from the residual common law powers of the Crown (the prerogative), as in the case itself, though they may not be applicable to such prerogative powers as the dissolution of Parliament or the granting of honours.

ILLEGALITY

Under the heading of illegality Lord Diplock said, 'the decision-maker must understand correctly the law that regulates his decision-making power and must give effect to it' (*GCHQ*, p. 1196). The difficulty is to distinguish a mistake of law that regulates the decision-making power (error going to jurisdiction) from a mistake of law which the decision-maker has the authority to determine (error of law). The distinction between the law which delimits the jurisdiction of the decision-maker and that which is within his jurisdiction was for practical purposes eliminated in the *Anisminic* case (1969) when a decision of the Foreign Compensation Commission, a body set up to distribute compensation for property expropriated abroad, was declared invalid for misconstruction of provisions it was supposed to interpret, although the decisions were expressly declared in the statute as not being open to challenge in any court. By holding that the decision of the Commission was void, the House of Lords set aside the exclusion clause. As a result of the decision any error of law of a decision-making body is open to judicial review. Taken to its logical conclusion this would enable the courts on an application for judicial review to sit in judgement on the interpretation of all the statutory provisions and those contained in delegated legislation which has been entrusted to the various types of decision-making bodies. In practice the courts have not used their powers to the full extent. They may categorize the error as one of fact rather than law where the words to be interpreted are ordinary, non-technical English words, and may leave their interpretation to be determined by the inferior body unless the interpretation is so unreasonable that no reasonable body could reach it, when it would fall within Lord Diplock's second ground of irrationality. The courts will also adopt this approach where they feel the question of interpretation is more suitable for an expert body, which has been set up by Parliament for this purpose, than for the courts. It is, however, very difficult to predict when the courts will adopt the hands-off approach and when they will reinterpret the relevant provisions themselves. This is where extra-legal considerations come into play and the attitude of the judiciary towards questions of social policy may be the hidden premise on which the decision is based.

The attitude of the courts towards issues of policy may be quite explicit when they lay down criteria which the decision-maker must take into account but which are not mentioned in the statutory provisions and may directly contradict statutory provisions which give wide discretionary powers to a body to act as it thinks fit. These limitations which the courts superimpose on statutory provisions may be explicitly designed to protect individual rights, e.g. not to be deprived of access to the courts. Thus the courts will, as we saw in the *Anisminic* case, construe any statutory provision to this effect as narrowly as possible, though even here the attitude is not consistent and they have held to be judge-proof clauses which exclude judicial control after six weeks, e.g. in the case of compulsory purchase orders, where a reopening of the decision would cause administrative chaos (*R v. Secretary of State for the Environment ex parte Ostler,* 1977). The courts will also narrowly construe a power to levy a charge from the citizen so that express provision is necessary and even wide discretionary powers will not be sufficient authorization. Thus a wide power to control food supplies under regulations made to secure the public safety and the defence of the realm did not include a power to charge for the issue of a licence to purchase milk (*AG v. Wiltshire United Dairies,* 1921), and a power to revoke a television licence by a notice in writing did not give the Home Secretary power to revoke a licence which had been renewed before the expiry of the old one so as to avoid paying the increased fee (*Congreve v. Home Office,* 1976).

Similarly the courts have construed legislation and wide discretionary powers exercised under it so as not to take away property rights. The attitude of the judiciary towards great issues of social policy such as slum clearance, council housing and town and country planning can be plotted according to how they have interpreted the legislation vis-à-vis the property owner. This has fluctuated from periods of intense hostility to the Housing Acts in the 1930s to a period of acquiescence in town and country planning legislation after 1945 until a reaction set in in the late 1950s when the courts reasserted private property rights in a spate of decisions which emasculated the Town and Country Planning Acts. Parliament engaged in a running battle with the courts at these times, amending the statutes so as to prevent the courts from misinterpreting the legislation, but the courts have the last word on interpretation. The courts can thus limit the ambit of social legislation by superimposing their policy conceptions based on individual rights when interpreting a statute.

Perhaps the most striking illustration of the courts reading limitations into statutory provisions so as to narrow the discretionary powers conferred under them is the duty the courts impose on local authorities to hold the balance between their ratepayers and other sections of the community. This was one of the grounds on which the GLC's Fares Fair policy, which cut London Transport's fares, was declared unlawful by the courts in *Bromley London Borough Council v. GLC* (1982). Similarly in 1925 in *Roberts v. Hopwood* it was held on the same principle unlawful for a local authority to exercise its powers to pay such wages as it thought fit by paying all its workers male and female a minimum of £4 a week, which was excessive by commercial standards at that time. In contrast the courts held in 1983 in *Pickwell v. Camden London Borough Council* that Camden Borough Council had not acted unlawfully when it settled a strike of manual workers by agreeing a figure above that at which a national settlement was later negotiated. The court said that it was not the basic legal principle which had changed but our attitudes. The real issue is whether the attitude of the courts should prevail over that of the elected local authority in exercising a discretionary power. In the *Camden* case, unlike the *GLC* case and *Roberts v. Hopwood*, the court bent over backwards not to interfere with the judgement of the elected body.

IRRATIONALITY

These cases can also be used as illustrations of Lord Diplock's second ground of judicial review in the *GCHQ* case (1984), i.e. irrationality, which he defines as unreasonableness in accordance with the principles of the *Wednesbury* case (1948), i.e. 'a decision which is so outrageous in its defiance of logic or of accepted moral standards that no sensible person who had applied his mind to the question to be decided could have arrived at it' (*GCHQ*, p. 1196). This principle was construed very narrowly in the *Camden* case so as not to interfere with the judgement of the local authority. However, in the *Secretary of State for Education v. Tameside Borough Council* (1977) the courts had the unenviable task of having to judge the unreasonableness of the decisions of two elected authorities, the minister and the local authority who were in conflict. The Secretary of State for Education had power to give a direction to a local authority which he was satisfied was acting unreasonably. He gave such a direction to the local authority who, after a local election which the Conservatives won, overturned the decision of their Labour predecessors to adopt comprehensive education and abolish grammar schools. The minister thought there was insufficient time to implement the new selection process before the beginning of the school year. The court applied the very narrow test of unreasonableness to the local authority's actions which had just been approved by the electorate. On the other hand, they held that the minister had no grounds for finding that the local authority had acted unreasonably and that no reasonable minister could so find. This seems to be applying differing tests of unreasonableness to the minister and the local authority. In contrast to this case the Secretary of State for the Environment was held to be acting reasonably when he used his default powers against Norwich City Council (*R v. Secretary of State for the Environment ex parte Norwich City Council*, 1982) because of their policy of passive resistance to the sale of council houses. As these cases illustrate, the courts have in recent years been used increasingly as the forum where the conflict between local and central government is being fought out. This has escalated in the area of local government finance where in case upon case the courts have been asked to interpret the complicated provisions of the successive statutes which tighten the financial noose round local authorities. In one of the most important of these cases which challenged the legality of the whole system of targets under the Local Government Finance Act 1982 (*R v. Secretary of State for the Environment ex parte Nottingham County Council*, 1986) the House of Lords, reversing the Court of Appeal, upheld the decision of the minister. Lord Scarman, with whom the rest of the court agreed, held that in this case, where the minister's decision had to be approved by the House of Commons, 'it is not for the judges to say that the action has such unreasonable consequences that the guidance upon which the action is based and of which the House of Commons had notice was perverse and must be set aside. For that is a question of policy for the minister and the Commons, unless there has been bad faith or misconduct by the minister' (pp. 7–8). Even more pointedly, Lord Bridge said, 'Judicial review is not just a move in an interminable chess tournament. Although I do not blame Nottingham or Bradford for instituting these proceedings, I hope that in future local authorities will bite on the bullet and not seek to persuade the courts to absolve them from compliance with the Secretary of State's guidance. If for any particular city or for any group of cities guidance is set too low, having regard to their peculiar needs, then persuasion should be offered not to the judges, who are not qualified to listen, but to the department, the minister, all members of parliament and ultimately to the electorate' (p. 23). This impeccable constitutional advice has, however, fallen on deaf ears and the challenge to the decision to rate-cap local authorities continues. When ministers refuse to give way, Parliament is whipped and the General Election is years ahead, the courts become the political arena because the political remedies do not work. This makes it very difficult for the judges to remain above the political battle, for even judicial abstention, as in the *Nottingham* case, can be seen as taking sides. In our constitution based on the sovereignty of Parliament it is a sign of breakdown of the political system when the courts are used as a political battleground.

PROCEDURAL IMPROPRIETY

Lord Diplock's third ground of judicial review is concerned with challenge to the procedure by which the decision is reached rather than with its substance. In practice this may often be the only line of attack open to an applicant who wants a decision to which he objects set aside, because he cannot challenge the decision on its merits by judicial review. The quashing of the decision may be a pyrrhic victory as a new decision may be taken after following the correct procedure but in many cases the victory will in practice be final.

The procedural impropriety may be the result of not following procedural rules laid down by statute or delegated legislation, though the courts will not construe every minor failure to observe such provisions as grounds for striking down such a decision.

Though most tribunals and public inquiries are regulated by procedural rules, many decisions made by ministers, local authorities and other public bodies are not regulated by statutory procedures. It is in this area that the courts have been most creative in fashioning principles to which those who make decisions affecting individuals must conform. The most famous principles are the rules of natural justice which have been applied to a constantly expanding area of decision-making. Though originally the courts distinguished these rules from the more flexible concept of procedural fairness, they are now often treated as synonymous, their application varying according to the subject-matter of the decision. Out of these rules the courts have now developed a new concept of procedural propriety where a legitimate expectation of the applicant is withdrawn.

There are two rules of natural justice which the courts have formulated, namely that no one may be a judge in his own cause and that a person affected by a decision must be given an opportunity to state his case and one person must not be heard behind the back of the other. These basic moral principles, allegedly derived from the Old Testament, have given rise to a myriad of cases to determine their application in a vast variety of situations.

The first rule of natural justice is a rule against bias in the decision-maker, who should have no personal or pecuniary interest in the decision. This rule, which, like its twin, is modelled on the judicial process, caused particular difficulty in relation to decisions of ministers who had to hold a public inquiry into objections against a decision made by themselves, e.g. to build a road or designate a new town, and ultimately had to decide whether to confirm their own decision after having heard the objectors. Bias in favour of their own decision was built into the decision-making process and the courts held in the famous case concerning Stevenage New Town, *Franklin v. Minister of Town and Country Planning* (1948), that so long as the minister gave genuine consideration to the objections raised at the inquiry he could be as biased in favour of building a new town at Stevenage as he liked. A minister making a policy decision could not be forced into the straitjacket of a judge.

Similar problems were encountered in applying the second rule of natural justice to ministerial decisions reached after public inquiries. In another landmark decision, *Local Government Board v. Arlidge* (1915), it was held that the inspector's report to the minister after the inquiry did not have to be disclosed. This decision has now been reversed by the statutory rules regulating the procedure of inquiries which are made under the Tribunals and Inquiries Act 1971. These regulations are a statutory embodiment of the rules of natural justice applicable to public inquiries but problems of their interpretation still have to be decided by the courts and, where an inquiry is not regulated by rules, they are still called upon to adapt the rules of natural justice to a policy decision reached by a judicialized procedure. Thus in *Bushell v. Secretary of State for the Environment* (1980) the House of Lords had to decide whether the methodology for making traffic predictions for a new road was a question of fact and therefore open to cross-examination or a matter of policy on which cross-examination was rightly disallowed. In deciding the latter they were very much influenced by the view that a motorway inquiry is part of the policy-making process rather than a trial.

The cases relating to public inquiries were regarded as in a special category by Lord Reid in *Ridge v. Baldwin* (1964), the case which was the springboard from which the expansion of natural justice took off. The courts had before that case limited the application of the rules of natural justice to deprivation of rights rather than privileges and had not applied them to the exercise of wide discretionary powers or the exercise of disciplinary functions. In *Ridge v. Baldwin* the House of Lords declared void the dismissal of the Chief Constable of Brighton because he had not been offered an opportunity to present his case, his dismissal being based on what he himself and the judge had said at his trial on a charge of corruption of which he was acquitted. The court brushed aside the decisions which had narrowed the application of natural justice and, basing itself on earlier decisions, held that where there must be something against a man before he could be dismissed from an office, as in this case, the rules of natural justice had to be observed.

The block having been removed, the way was open to apply the rules of natural justice to an ever expanding category of cases. One of these has been university students who have been held entitled to the benefit of the rules of natural justice before having their course terminated (*R v. Aston University ex parte Roffey*, 1969) or being suspended from the university (*Glynn v. Keele University*, 1971), although in both cases the courts refused a remedy in the exercise of their discretion because of the facts of the cases. More recently the courts have broken open the prison gates and applied the rules of natural justice in favour of prisoners, at least in the case of the hearing of the more serious charges against discipline before a Board of Visitors in the prison (*R v. Visitors of Hull Prison ex parte St Germain*, 1979). They drew a distinction between such cases and the hearing of the less serious cases before the governor of the prison, whose function was said to be analogous to the commanding officer dispensing military discipline and the schoolmaster dealing with school discipline. The rules of natural justice also have a very limited part to play in the decisions to grant parole to prisoners and, where issues of national security are involved, the courts have refused to apply them, e.g. in the case of a deportation order based on this ground (*R v. Home Secretary ex parte Hosenball,* 1977).

The courts have also varied the content of the rules in accordance with the circumstances of the case. They can include the duty to give reasons, the right to legal representation and the right to cross-examine witnesses at an oral hearing or merely an opportunity to make representations without knowing all the evidence against one or the source of the information. This attenuated form of natural justice is sometimes referred to as a duty to act fairly but these terms are also treated as synonymous. Recently the duty to act fairly has been applied to cases where a person has a 'legitimate expectation'. This vague concept has been applied to a number of situations such as the revocation of a permit before it has expired, the remission of a sentence and, as we saw, the statement in a Home Office circular of the circumstances when an adopted child would be allowed into this country. The most famous application of the concept was in the *GCHQ* case when the House of Lords held that the trade unions at GCHQ had a legitimate expectation based on past practice to be consulted about the ban on employees from being members of a trade union. This right to be consulted was, however, in the circumstances of the case negated in the interests of national security. But it was successfully asserted in one of the many cases concerning local government finance, enabling a number of London borough councils to have the decision reducing their grant declared invalid because the minister had refused to hear further representations (*R v. Secretary of State for the Environment ex parte Brent LBC*, 1982). The victory was pyrrhic for one authority because the minister, having listened to further representations, still withheld the grant (*R v. Secretary of State for the Environment ex parte Hackney LBC*, 1983). The concept of legitimate expectation has extended the principle of fairness to a category of cases where natural justice had not previously been applied and has thus advanced the cause of open government, though at the expense of slowing down the process of policy-making. This is the inevitable price to be paid for greater participation in decision-making and, if the concept of legitimate expectation is carried to its logical conclusion, it may become too high a cost.

A legitimate expectation giving a right to natural justice may also arise from an express promise, but the promise is not binding as such. The courts have evolved a principle of public law which says that a public authority cannot fetter the exercise of its discretionary powers by a promise to act in a particular way even if this has been relied upon to his detriment by the person to whom the promise is made. A public authority must be able to change its policy in the public interest even at the expense of a private individual. Thus it was held in *Laker Airways Ltd v. Department of Trade* (1977) that the government was entitled to change its policy about the licence granted to Mr Laker to run Skytrain to the USA, even though he had suffered loss by relying on previous representations, because a government must be allowed to change its policy (Lord Denning dissented on this point). However, the government's policy decision was declared invalid on other grounds.

Similarly, a government may not fetter its own discretion by laying down rules for its exercise unless it is prepared to hear representations from anyone that the rule should be changed or not apply to him. This ensures that discretion is exercised on the facts of each case and was another ground on which the London borough councils won their case against the reduction of their grant, for the minister had refused to listen to any further representations. This rule is the converse of the legitimate expectation rule which prevents the public authority from changing its mind without first giving those affected an opportunity to make representations. One rule is in favour of flexibility, the other is in favour of the status quo.

Thus the courts have fashioned a battery of principles through which they can impose their values on public authorities. The government can by legislation reverse any decision of the courts but it cannot easily eradicate the principles on which judicial control is based. Perhaps this should be regarded as the true meaning of the rule of law.

PARLIAMENTARY COMMISSIONER FOR ADMINISTRATION

The Parliamentary Commissioner for Administration (PCA) or Ombudsman, as he is popularly called, was set up under the Parliamentary Commissioner Act 1967 in response to pressure which began in 1954 with the Crichel Down affair, the classic illustration of maladministration by civil servants, for which the only remedy was to bring political and parliamentary pressure on the minister who eventually set up an inquiry to investigate the affair, which, as we saw, led to his resignation. Since this machinery cannot be set in motion for every mistake made in a government department, an aggrieved individual is left without a remedy apart from writing to his MP. The Franks Committee, which was set up in the wake of the Crichel Down affair, was only empowered to consider the workings of tribunals and inquiries and did not, therefore, include the ordinary administrative process of a government department. The catalyst which gave the impetus for the establishment of the PCA was a report commissioned in 1961 by JUSTICE, a private organization consisting of lawyers, which remodelled the Scandinavian institution of the Ombudsman by reference to the British Comptroller and Auditor General and recommended the creation of a Parliamentary Commissioner for Administration.

The hallmark of the PCA which distinguishes his office from that of the Ombudsman is its parliamentary nature. This is the rationale which underlies the whole institution and gives it its distinctive flavour. It is responsible for one of the main limitations peculiar to the British institution, namely that complaints must come through an MP rather than directly from the aggrieved citizen. This has not prevented individuals from approaching the PCA directly and he receives about the same number of complaints by this route as through MPs (i.e. about eight hundred annually). The PCA can now offer to send such cases to the MP, who can then ask him to investigate, but this procedure has only been used in a small proportion of cases because most of these complaints fall outside the PCA's jurisdiction (HC 615, 1977-8: Report of Select Committee on the PCA).

The narrowness of the PCA's jurisdiction is probably the greatest limitation on the office. The complaint must be one of maladministration resulting in injustice in connection with action taken by a government department or other body to which the Act applies, provided it is not in one of the excepted categories listed in the Act. Large areas of administration are thus excluded from the PCA's remit, though the gaps may be filled by other institutions. Thus the exclusion of local authorities is now made good by the establishment of Local Commissioners for Administration in 1974 who perform similar functions vis-à-vis local authorities. Complaints against the police are now supervised by the Police Complaints Authority set up under the Police and Criminal Evidence Act 1984. The PCA himself has been appointed as Health Service Commissioner, who since 1973 performs similar functions to the PCA in relation to the National Health Service. Governments have rejected the extension of the PCA's ambit to the nationalized industries on the grounds that they are commercial bodies and have their own complaints machinery. The government in 1985 accepted recommendations to include about fifty quangos within the PCA's jurisdiction including such bodies as the British Council, the Commission for Racial Equality and Equal Opportunities Commission and the London Docklands Development Corporation, thus increasing the public accountability of these bodies (Parliamentary and Health Service Commissioners Bill 1987).

Some of the excluded categories of cases have also been the subject of controversy, in particular the exclusion of personnel matters in relation to the armed forces and civil servants. Governments have steadfastly refused to extend the PCA's jurisdiction to these cases on the grounds that other employees do not have access to the PCA for their grievances and that there are other mechanisms available for their redress. The other controversial exclusion is for contractual and other commercial transactions. This excludes the whole area of government contracting, even though this has been used for political purposes as happened when the government blacklisted and refused to give government contracts to those firms which broke its incomes policy from 1975 to 1978. It also bars him from investigating the giving of assistance to industry under wide discretionary powers but includes within his remit assistance which applicants expect to receive (Cmnd 7449, 1979).

The arguments for exclusion in such cases became confused with the main limitation on the PCA's jurisdiction which prevents him questioning the merits of a decision taken without maladministration (Parliamentary Commissioner Act 1967, section 12(3)). Maladministration is not defined in the Act but Mr Crossman when introducing the Bill said it included bias, neglect, inattention, delay, incompetence, ineptitude, perversity, turpitude, arbitrariness. More succinctly, the first PCA drew the distinction between the processes by which the decision was reached and the quality of the decision itself (HC 6, 1967–8). Nevertheless, the distinction is a fine one and it was further blurred by his following the recommendation of the select committee, to whom he reports, which wanted him to exercise jurisdiction over a perverse decision and where an administrative rule led to hardship (HC 350, 1967–8). Some of the PCA's most famous cases have been on the borderline between maladministration and the merits of a decision. Among his first cases were British prisoners of war who had been kept in German concentration camps and had been refused compensation provided by the German government and distributed by the Foreign Office. The view had been taken that they did not fall within the rules which had been drawn up by the Foreign Office for its distribution. The PCA criticized this decision (HC 54, 1967–8) and the complainants were granted compensation by George Brown, the Foreign Secretary at the time, but he rejected the PCA's criticisms and questioned whether the PCA's judgement was better than that of all the Foreign Secretaries who had dealt with the problem (HC Deb., vol. 758, col. 115, 5 February 1968). Similarly, in the case of Court Line, a company which was given financial assistance by Mr Benn, the PCA criticized the wording of the minister's statement to the House of Commons about the company as misleading (HC 498, 1974–5). Again this criticism was rejected by the minister because these were issues of policy on which the government had to make a judgement rather than the PCA (HC Deb., vol. 897, col. 582, 6 August 1975). These cases show the danger of the PCA stepping outside his jurisdiction and becoming embroiled in highly controversial political issues. The risk is that he then becomes a political football who is used by the opposition to attack the government but whose reports are in consequence rejected by the government as not being within his terms of reference.

This weakens his position which is based on acceptance of his reports, not on enforcement. The PCA has no powers except to make reports. The report on the individual case is sent to the MP who forwarded the complaint and to the Department and individual who were the subject of the complaint. An annual report and now quarterly reports with selected cases are made to the House of

Commons where they are referred to the Select Committee on the PCA. Special reports may be made on *causes célèbres* such as the case of the prisoners of war (*Sachsenhausen* case) and the *Court Line* case. The only back-up power the PCA has, if he thinks that an injustice has not been remedied following his report, is to make a special report to the House of Commons (1967 Act, section 10(3)). This has happened in only one case so far (HC 598, 1977–8) on which the PCA had to back-track later (HC 91, 1978–9). This does not mean, as we have seen in the *Court Line* case, that his recommendations are always accepted, though this does happen in the vast majority of cases. It does, however, illustrate that the PCA gets his way through persuasion and sometimes negotiation with the Department, which may change its mind during the course of the investigation.

The Select Committee on the PCA, which was set up by the House of Commons and survived the reorganization of select committees in 1979, plays an important part in bringing pressure to bear on government departments. It does not reinvestigate individual cases but considers the annual and special reports of the PCA by questioning the departments which are most frequently complained against, i.e. the Department of Health and Social Security and the Inland Revenue. It monitors the extent to which complaints have been remedied and how far defects of administration highlighted in the reports have been put right. It is also concerned with reviewing the jurisdiction of the PCA and, as we have seen, has brought about important extensions of his terms of reference. It forms the most important pressure group for the PCA, though it has recently, and exceptionally, criticized the PCA himself for delay in handling a complaint, which, ironically, is one of the classic illustrations of maladministration (HC 312, 1985–6).

The average time taken for the investigation of complaints is twelve months, a figure which conceals enormous variations between individual complaints. Delay is largely the result of the PCA's method of investigation which has been described as a Rolls-Royce method. When the PCA decides to investigate, which he only does in about two hundred cases annually, as most cases referred to him fall outside his jurisdiction, his staff conduct a very thorough investigation through interviews and by examining departmental files. His powers of investigation are very wide. He has power to call for information from the minister downwards and he has access to all documents except those relating to the Cabinet (1967 Act, section 8). The thoroughness of his investigations accounts for the size of his staff (about one hundred) which is much greater than that of other ombudsmen. The composition of his staff, some of whom are seconded from the Civil Service, as well as their working methods, are again modelled on the Comptroller and Auditor General's office. Unlike other ombudsmen, the PCA has no lawyers on his staff, although the last two PCAs have themselves been lawyers in contrast to their predecessors who were civil servants.

The parliamentary connection of the PCA profoundly affects the publicity for his office and, therefore, his public image. His individual reports are not given to the press but to the MPs who may decide to inform the press. Very few of his cases have become headline news and the PCA himself is hardly a public figure. Whether this is to be regretted or applauded depends on one's perception of his function. The fact that he has unearthed no major scandal even of Crichel Down proportions may be an indication of the quality of the Civil Service or of the narrowness of his remit. He cannot disclose information obtained for the purpose of his investigation for any other purpose, e.g. to the police (1967 Act, section 11(2)). To change this was said by the then Head of the Civil Service to represent a major change of principle (HC 615, 1977–8, para. 35). He has no power, unlike his counterparts abroad, to make an investigation on his own initiative without a complaint. He is not a trouble-shooter who is asked by the government to investigate major issues of public concern, as again happens elsewhere. There are other mechanisms for this purpose, particularly tribunals of inquiry and select committees which sit in public to hear evidence. He cannot, like the courts, quash a decision or order the payment of damages, though in many cases he has secured *ex gratia* compensation for the complainant. He cannot deal with cases where there is a legal remedy unless he is satisfied that it is not reasonable to expect the complainant to resort to it (1967 Act, section 5(2)). He told Mr Evans, the former editor of *The Times*, who wanted him to investigate its sale to Mr Murdoch which had not been referred to the Monopolies Commission, that this was a political issue which was not within his powers of investigation (*Guardian*, 16 February 1984). When he does get drawn into a politically controversial issue he must, as we have seen, tread the tightrope between maladministration and merits. His main function in such cases, if he does investigate, is to establish the facts impartially, for which he has unparalleled powers. Perhaps the PCA's main importance is that he exists. As he pointed out in one of his reports, 'Those who are inclined to criticize our public service rather freely would do well to consider what it must be like to live in countries where to criticize a great department of state may be to invite imprisonment or worse' (HC 322, 1983–4, para. 1).

ACCOUNTABILITY TO PARLIAMENT

It could be said that there is not one ombudsman but 650, in that every MP acts as one, or 24,000 if one includes local councillors who perform similar functions in relation to local authorities. It has been estimated that MPs take up about a hundred thousand cases with ministers annually (HC 615, 1977–8, para. 6). As we have seen, only a very small proportion (less than 1 per cent) are referred to the PCA for investigation. Most MPs try to get the problems of their constituents solved by their own efforts and only refer cases which are too difficult for them or in order to placate their constituents. The PCA has suggested that it might be desirable if the citizen could ask the PCA directly to investigate, if he is dissatisfied with the ultimate response from his MP (HC 322, 1983–4, para. 7). The MP will normally first write a letter to the relevant authority. If correspondence does not lead to a solution he can then ask a parliamentary question. There are certain restrictions on the asking of questions. Ministers can only be asked about matters which fall within the sphere of their responsibility (HC 393, 1971–2). This has caused problems in relation to the nationalized industries. Under the nationalization legislation ministers only have certain powers and are not responsible for day-to-day matters. Even where questions of detail are technically in order, e.g. under the power to obtain information from the boards, a minister can refuse to answer and thus prevent the question being asked again for a period of time. The problem of asking questions on detail has been circumvented by phrasing the question in terms of asking the minister to give a general direction about the issue at hand, but even this bars questions about particular complaints such as the lateness of a certain train. Ministers can always deflect the question as falling within the responsibility of the board if it is on a day-to-day matter. Similar problems arise with regard to companies in which the government holds a stake. Ministers will answer questions on matters for which they accept responsibility, e.g. the appointment of directors, but not on matters of day-to-day management which are the responsibility of the firm, e.g. the sale of computers to South Africa by ICL in 1973. But where the minister himself has intervened, as in the request to Rolls-Royce (1971) Ltd (whose shares are owned by the government) to cancel its contracts with Chile in 1974, he must answer questions put to him. When ministers said that they would not vote their shareholding in privatized companies such as British Aerospace, they were told that they could not disclaim responsibility for a stake which they still owned then and had the power to use (HC Deb., vol. 974, col. 70, 19 November 1979). The Westland affair shows that they can certainly not disclaim responsibility for interventions which they do in fact make, provided, of course, that this becomes known. The same rules apply to other quangos over which the minister retains limited powers. Thus ministers will refuse to answer questions about programmes broadcast by the BBC or even the use of their reserve powers in this respect, though this has not prevented great public controversy where there has been open pressure brought to bear on the BBC. MPs may also raise grievances on the adjournment debates at the end of each day's sitting and on the other days set aside for backbenchers, e.g. debates on the annual Appropriation Bills and the debates on the adjournment of the House for a specified period such as at Christmas.

Financial accountability to Parliament is through the Comptroller and Auditor General (C & AG) who reports to the Public Accounts Committee. The C & AG audits the accounts of government departments and some quangos and is concerned not just with whether money has been spent legally, i.e. in accordance with the Appropriation Act, but whether it has been used economically and efficiently, though he may not question the merits of government policy. On the basis of his reports the Public Accounts Committee questions officials from the Department and in particular the

Permanent Secretary who is personally accountable for the expenditure of public money. The political responsibility of the minister is, however, paramount, so that if the Permanent Secretary considers a minister's decision financially irregular or imprudent he must place his objection on record but in the last resort carry out the minister's instructions (HC 393, 1971–2, Q. 133).

Governments of both political parties have always resisted allowing the C & AG access to the accounts of the nationalized industries because they argue that this would hinder their freedom to act as commercial bodies. As we have seen, this freedom is much hampered already by ministerial control and it is the desire to preserve accountability to ministers and through them to Parliament which is probably the real stumbling block to granting the C & AG access to the accounts. Similarly, he has no access to the accounts of limited companies in which the government owns some or all of the shares or to whom it gives subsidies. Where public money has been lost, as in the case of the De Lorean car firm in Northern Ireland, he has no access to the accounts of the company, but only to those of the government department, whom he and the Public Accounts Committee can criticize for not monitoring the firm sufficiently (HC 127, 1983–4). Again accountability is through the minister and not directly to Parliament. The select committees which oversee government departments also monitor the nationalized industries and government-owned firms such as Rolls-Royce and British Leyland but such examinations, unlike those of the Public Accounts Committee, are not based on detailed investigation of the accounts of the departments.

In contrast the accounts of local authorities are audited by auditors appointed by the Audit Commission, a body set up by the Local Government Finance Act 1982. Before that date they were appointed by the minister. The auditor can apply to the court for a declaration that the expenditure of a local authority was unlawful (section 19). In view of the principles applied by the courts to local authorities, such an issue may be highly politically controversial, with the courts declaring unlawful expenditure for which councillors had a mandate from the electorate. Even more controversial is the power to order councillors to repay the money so spent or wrongfully lost and to disqualify them from office, as happened in

Liverpool and Lambeth as a result of the rate-setting rebellion. This gives rise to a conflict between legal and political responsibility which is avoided at the level of central government.

None of the mechanisms of control and accountability so far examined involves those who are directly affected by the decisions. There are some institutions designed for this purpose but they have a rather low profile. The consumer councils established for the nationalized industries to hear complaints and represent the consumer interest are not generally regarded as very effective. Community health councils set up to monitor the National Health Service when it was reorganized in 1973 are in a similar position. Neighbourhood councils sprang up spontaneously in deprived inner city areas to represent the views of the community but they have never been put on a statutory basis as was recommended by the Royal Commission on Local Government in 1969 (Cmnd 4040, Chapter IX). The climate of the times is not very favourable to grass roots democracy but this might change radically under a different government.

5

Civil Liberties and a Bill of Rights

Dicey (1885, p. 195) gave as his third meaning of the Rule of Law, 'that the constitution is pervaded by the rule of law on the ground that the general principles of the constitution (as, for example, the right to personal liberty, or the right of public meeting) are with us the result of judicial decisions determining the rights of private persons in particular cases brought before the courts; whereas under many foreign constitutions the security (such as it is) given to the rights of individuals results, or appears to result, from the general principles of the constitution.' What Dicey regarded as the strength of the constitution so far as civil liberties were concerned is now criticized as one of its weaknesses and has given rise to the call for the enactment of a Bill of Rights modelled on the European Convention for the Protection of Human Rights and Fundamental Freedoms. In order to see how this *volte face* has come about, we will examine how the civil liberties mentioned by Dicey are protected under English law and how they would be safeguarded if a Bill of Rights enacting the European Convention on Human Rights were passed.

PERSONAL LIBERTY

Under this heading are usually included freedom from unlawful arrest and detention and unlawful search of one's person or premises and the seizure of one's property. It is no longer true to say as Dicey did that the rights of the individual in this area are the result of judicial decisions because the Police and Criminal Evidence Act 1984 now embodies the law on this subject and judicial decisions will now have to interpret the Act and the codes made under it rather than follow previous decisions. It is to this Act, therefore, that we must look for the powers of the police to arrest and detain individuals, to search their person and premises and to seize property. The Act and judicial decisions lay down the limitations on personal liberty, they do not state the rights of the individual. This is the crucial difference from the European Convention on Human Rights. The rights in English law are implicit, it is the limitations of those rights which must be authorized by law. Dicey saw this as an important element of the rule of law, first because the focus is on the remedy by which the rights are safeguarded rather than the rights themselves. He took as his example the remedy of habeas corpus. Historically this was of profound significance but, though the right to apply for habeas corpus is expressly saved by the 1984 Act (section 51(d)), its scope is subject to the provisions of that Act. Secondly, Dicey pointed out that constitutions containing declarations of rights may be suspended and, similarly, the European Convention on Human Rights (except for certain articles) can be derogated from in time of war or other public emergency threatening the life of the nation (article 15). On the other hand, the rights of the individual in Britain cannot be abrogated by a stroke of the pen, though an individual remedy such as habeas corpus has been suspended in time of war or emergency.

However, virtually the same result as the suspension of constitutional rights can come about by an Act of Parliament giving wide powers to the government in time of war or emergency to make regulations to secure the public safety and defence of the realm or the supply and distribution of the necessities of life. In both World Wars the government made regulations under these Acts empowering it to detain persons whom it reasonably believed to be of hostile origin and associations, which in effect deprived such persons of the right to habeas corpus (*Liversidge v. Anderson*, 1942). It is, therefore, the substantive law which limits the freedom of the individual and the remedies by which he can protect his freedom which determine the extent of his liberty. The extent to which these would be affected by the enactment of a Bill of Rights will be considered later.

Arrest and detention

The Police and Criminal Evidence Act 1984 extended the powers of the police to arrest suspects. The power of summary arrest by a police constable applied to reasonable suspicion of an offence punishable with imprisonment for five years (arrestable offences) and in addition to a number of less serious offences where there were specific statutory provisions for arrest. There was also a common law power of arrest for breach of the peace. The Act has widened the category of arrestable offences by adding certain offences which are not punishable with five years' imprisonment (section 24). But more importantly it now gives a power of summary arrest in the case of *any* offence provided certain conditions are satisfied. These are concerned either with the inability to ascertain the correct name or a satisfactory address of the suspect so that it will be impracticable to bring the person before a court by issuing a summons, or with the prevention of serious mischief such as physical injury to himself or others or loss or damage to property. But the latter grounds also include preventing the commission of an offence against public decency and obstruction of the highway, which gives the police a wide discretion (section 25). The provisions in the Act are peppered with the phrase 'has reasonable grounds' for suspecting or doubting or believing. The reasonableness of the grounds can only be tested afterwards by an action for damages for false imprisonment. Similarly, a person must be told both that he is under arrest and the grounds for his arrest; the arrest is not lawful otherwise (section 28). But again this can only be tested afterwards in an action for damages. Persons who are voluntarily helping the police with their inquiries are free to leave unless arrested (section 29) but there are no provisions for telling persons this except at the stage when they are suspected of an offence (Code, para. 3.9).

The use of powers of arrest varies greatly between police forces. In *Mohammed-Holgate v. Duke* (1984), an action for wrongful arrest, it was argued that it was unlawful to arrest someone, even if he was reasonably suspected of an arrestable offence, if he was only arrested so that greater pressure could be put on him to confess than if he were interviewed without being arrested. The House of Lords held that, since the police officer had a discretion whether to arrest, once he had reasonable grounds for suspecting an arrestable offence, the exercise of his discretion could not be questioned except on grounds of irrationality (see Chapter 4). This case sanctioned the power of the police to arrest and detain suspects for questioning, provided that there was a power to arrest, before this was explicitly enshrined in the 1984 Act, section 37.

It is now recognized that the primary purpose of detaining a person in police custody after arrest is to obtain from him or through him sufficient evidence to charge him with an offence. The Act and the code made under it are an attempt to hold the balance between giving the police powers to hold the suspect and question him and safeguarding the rights of the individual. Whether the balance is tipped too far in one direction or the other is a matter of judgement that can only be reached after examining the provisions. There is much dispute whether the provisions increased the powers of the police before the Act but the answer is inconclusive because the powers were so uncertain, which was one of the main reasons for passing the Act. The Act and the code are a mixture of police powers and safeguards for the individual, the crucial issue is the extent to which the safeguards are enforceable.

Where the police do not have sufficient evidence to charge the arrested person they may detain him for questioning for up to twenty-four hours with reviews by a superior officer after six hours and nine hours thereafter. At the end of that period he must either be charged with an offence or released (section 41). However, in the case of a serious arrestable offence which is rather widely defined in the Act (section 116), the period of detention can be extended up to thirty-six hours and this can be extended by a magistrates' court for two further periods of up to thirty-six hours to a maximum of ninety-six hours (sections 42–44). This maximum period is longer than that allowed by any common law country but it must be set against the statistics obtained by the Royal Commission on Criminal Procedure (Cmnd 8092, 1981, para. 3.96) that 75 per cent of all suspects are dealt with in six hours and 95 per cent within twenty-four hours; only 0.4 per cent were found to have been held for seventy-two hours or more. The limits on detention can be enforced by habeas corpus if the practical problems of making an application for the writ can be overcome and an action for damages for wrongful detention could be brought afterwards. The remedies to enforce the other safeguards are not so clear.

When a person is arrested he is given into the charge of a custody officer, who must be of the rank of sergeant or above and who is responsible for ensuring that persons in detention are treated in accordance with the Act and the code made under it (sections 36 and 39) and that a custody record is kept for each person in accordance with the provisions of the Act and the code which lay down what must be recorded, when and by whom. This is to ensure that the procedures laid down are followed correctly and that the safeguards for the treatment of individuals are being observed. But failure to observe these provisions would not make the detention unlawful. Failure to observe the Act or the code renders the police officer liable to disciplinary proceedings (section 67) but there is no independent investigation of complaints against the police, though the Act establishes an independent body, the Police Complaints Authority, to supervise the investigation of complaints (Part IX). There are, however, other safeguards in the Act and the code.

The Act (section 56) gives a person detained in custody the right on request to have someone of his choice informed that he is being detained. This right can be delayed for up to thirty-six hours in the case of a person detained for a serious arrestable offence if there are reasonable grounds for fearing that evidence will be interfered with or other suspects will be alerted. Under the code he must be informed of this right. More importantly the Act (section 58) gives a right to a detained person to consult a solicitor privately on request. Again this right may be delayed for up to thirty-six hours for the same reasons, and again under the code he must be informed of this right. Studies done for the Royal Commission indicated that before the Act, when the right was not statutory, few suspects asked to see a solicitor and most seem to have been refused their request, but they also found that few police forces took adequate steps to make suspects aware of their rights (Cmnd 8092, 1981, para. 4.83). Perhaps the most important change made by the Act is the extension of the duty solicitor scheme to police stations, so that free legal advice will be available round the clock to suspects, though there are limits to the amount of advice available under the scheme. Under the code a person may not be interviewed until he has received legal advice, where he has requested it, except where the thirty-six-hour delay applies or he has agreed in writing or where it would unreasonably delay the investigation, which gives further discretion to the police. The solicitor must also be allowed to be present at the interview.

These are important safeguards to prevent improper pressure being brought upon the suspect, provided that they can be enforced. When the Act was being implemented on a trial basis before it came into force, juveniles detained after the Tottenham riot in 1985 were prevented from seeing either their parents or solicitors. In *R v. Lemsatef* (1977), a case decided before the Act, it was held that where a suspect was wrongly denied access to a solicitor in breach of the non-statutory Judges' Rules, which then applied, the confession obtained from the accused was nevertheless admissible and the conviction could not be quashed on this ground. Since the Act a confession would not be admissible where it was obtained by oppression or where anything was said or done which was likely to render it unreliable (section 76). Mere breach of the provisions of the Act or the code would seem not to fall within the section; but the judge declared inadmissible the confessions of juveniles charged after the Tottenham riot, because of the conduct of the police (*Guardian*, 25 February and 11 March 1987). So far as evidence other than confessions is concerned, it will only be inadmissible under the Act if having regard to all the circumstances, including the way it was obtained, it would have such an adverse effect on the fairness of the proceedings that the court should not admit it (section 78). Again it would seem that breach of the Act and the code would not by itself suffice to exclude the evidence.

Arguably the most important safeguards for suspects contained in the Act are still at the experimental stage. Section 60 of the Act lays a duty on the Home Secretary to require interviews of suspects to be tape-recorded. Field trials are being held which were expected to take two years to complete. When tape-recording is finally introduced it should be a considerable safeguard but once again breach of the duty to tape-record interviews will not as such render the evidence inadmissible.

Thus the Act contains extensions of police powers to arrest and detain suspects but it also has impressive safeguards. The difficulty lies in enforcing them. The main sanction will be disciplinary proceedings against the police officer, so ultimately the Act relies to a great extent on the police policing themselves.

Stop and search power

There is power under the Act (Part I) to stop and search persons and vehicles in a public place on reasonable suspicion of finding stolen goods or offensive weapons. This power previously existed only in certain areas of the country which had obtained special legislation in private Acts of Parliament. It is a very controversial power which has had particular impact on some sections of the community such as young black people and which Lord Scarman pinpointed as a contributory factor in sparking off the Brixton disorders (Cmnd 8427, 1981, para. 3.27). The code of practice on stop and search powers now lays down guidance on what does and does not constitute reasonable suspicion and states explicitly that colour or style of dress can never by themselves be grounds for reasonable suspicion. But breach of the code is not a crime nor does it give rise to an action for damages by itself, though it must be taken into account in any proceedings to which it is relevant (section 67), which would be an action for assault where the stop and search was unlawful.

Search and seizure

The other main police power under the Act is to enter and search premises and seize property. From a historical point of view this is perhaps the greatest infringement of individual liberty because the great constitutional case proclaimed in ringing tones the principle that an Englishman's home is his castle, 'The great end, for which men entered into society, was to secure their property' (*Entick v. Carrington*, 1765). This eighteenth-century case decided that it was illegal for the Home Secretary to issue a warrant authorizing entry of a person's house to search for and seize his papers to find evidence of seditious libel. Since that case was decided, the power to search for evidence of an offence or for unlawful articles was conferred by a number of statutes, but there were glaring gaps such as the lack of a power to issue a search warrant to find evidence in the case of murder. This was highlighted in the case of *Ghani v. Jones*

(1970) where the police managed to obtain the passports and letters from persons they suspected of being implicated in a murder but were ordered to hand them back by Lord Denning because they had not shown reasonable grounds for believing that the plaintiffs were implicated in the crime or that the documents were material evidence to prove commission of the crime. In that case Lord Denning laid down sweeping propositions of law about search and seizure of property for which there was little authority. This confused and haphazard state of the law cried out for reform which is now embodied in the 1984 Act.

The Act for the first time gave a general power to the police to obtain a warrant from a magistrate to enter premises and to search for evidence where they have reasonable grounds to believe that a serious arrestable offence has been committed and that this was the only practicable way to obtain the evidence (section 8). The premises may be those of a third party who is not suspected of any offence. When the Bill was first published there was an outcry from the caring professions, e.g. doctors and social workers, who feared the possibility of their confidential records being ransacked to find evidence of a crime. As a result the second Bill was substantially modified so as to exclude from its ambit altogether confidential personal records as well as confidential journalistic material in addition to communications between a client and his legal adviser which had been previously excluded. Other confidential or journalistic material can only be searched for by obtaining an order from a circuit judge (section 9).

No warrant or order is necessary to search the premises in which a person was arrested (section 32) or to search the premises occupied by someone arrested for an arrestable offence after his arrest (section 18) for evidence relating to that offence. Once lawfully on the premises, the police may take anything which they reasonably believe is evidence of any offence whatsoever in order to prevent the evidence being lost or destroyed (section 19). These provisions put into statutory form some of the most controversial statements made by Lord Denning in *Ghani v. Jones* (1970) and even go beyond them. They encourage the police to go on fishing expeditions, looking for evidence which is not within the warrant or is not connected with the offence for which a person is arrested. Though such searches may be illegal under the provisions of the Act (sections 16(8), 18(3) and 32(3)), evidence so found would not be inadmissible unless it fell within the provision for the exclusion of unfair evidence (section 78). The Royal Commission would have excluded evidence obtained by an illegal search (Cmnd 8092, para. 3.49) to minimize fishing expeditions. The possibility of an action for damages after the event against the police and possible disciplinary proceedings are not a sufficient deterrent. The Englishman's castle has let down its draw-bridge for the police.

Telephone tapping and surveillance

The police have other means of obtaining evidence of an offence which are subject to even fewer safeguards than is the searching of premises. Telephone tapping was, until April 1986, when the Inter-ception of Communications Act 1985 came into force, carried out under the authority of a warrant issued by a Secretary of State in accordance with guidelines which had been laid down by him. When the legality of this procedure was challenged in *Malone v. Metro-politan Police Commissioner* (1979) the judge did not follow *Entick v. Carrington* (1765) and hold such warrants illegal because no property right was infringed by telephone tapping. He held that 'it can lawfully be done simply because there is nothing to make it unlawful' (pp. 733–4). The principle, which can be regarded as an important safeguard for the rights of the individual, had a dia-metrically opposite result here. *Malone* took his case to the Euro-pean Court of Human Rights (1984) where it was held that the United Kingdom had broken the European Convention on Human Rights, Article 8, under which everyone has the right to respect for his private and family life, his home and his correspondence. The court held that the minimum degree of legal protection to which citizens are entitled under the rule of law in a democratic society was lacking. To comply with the judgement, the Interception of Com-munications Act 1985 was passed by Parliament. This makes tele-phone tapping a criminal offence except where it is carried out by consent or under the authority of a warrant issued by the Secretary of State in accordance with the provisions of the Act (section 1). The Act now lays down in broad terms the grounds on which warrants may be issued, their scope and duration and the procedure for issuing them, as well as other safeguards (sections 2–6). A tribunal of lawyers has been set up to whom complaint can be made by someone who thinks his telephone has been tapped, but they can only investigate whether there has been a warrant issued and whether this complies with the Act (section 7). They cannot investigate illegal tapping without a warrant, for which a prosecution can be brought only with the consent of the Director of Public Prosecutions. The decisions of the tribunal cannot be challenged in any court (section 7) nor can any proceedings be brought before a court challenging the legality of a warrant or the legality of telephone tapping except where there is a prosecution for illegal tapping (section 9). It would, therefore, now be impossible for someone in the position of *Malone* to bring his case before a court. It was, however, possible for the Campaign for Nuclear Disarmament (CND) to challenge the legality of a warrant allegedly issued by the Home Secretary to tap the phone of its vice-president before the Act came into force (*Guardian*, 3 September 1986). The judge rejected the application because he held that the warrant had been lawfully issued on grounds of national security. He held that he could review the case even though it involved a question of national security and went on to hold that in accordance with the doctrine of legitimate expectation (see Chapter 4) ministers were bound by their own guidelines.

Guidelines issued by the Home Secretary to police forces on the use of other forms of surveillance are still the only restrictions on the use of such devices, and the guidelines only came to light accidentally (HC Deb., vol. 18, col. 452, Written Answers, 25 February 1982).

FREEDOM OF SPEECH AND PUBLIC ASSEMBLY

Dicey said of the right to free speech, 'Freedom of discussion is then, in England, little else than the right to write or say anything which a jury consisting of twelve shopkeepers think it expedient should be said or written' (p. 246). He was, of course, referring to the law of libel. But Dicey was mainly concerned in his discussion of freedom of speech to contrast freedom of the press in Britain with that in

France. His basic argument was that the press in Britain was subject to the ordinary law of the land and there was no special press law providing for censorship or giving the press special privileges. In essence that is true today, though, as we have seen, journalistic material is given a special status under the Police and Criminal Evidence Act 1984. Journalists, having obtained these special provisions, later had second thoughts for the reasons given by Dicey, because it singled them out for special treatment.

There are many other legal restrictions on freedom of speech both at common law and by statute apart from the law of libel. The notorious section 2 of the Official Secrets Act 1911 under which Clive Ponting was unsuccessfully prosecuted is perhaps at the moment the most criticized limitation. Increasingly today individuals want to exercise freedom of speech not in isolation but together with their fellow citizens in marches and demonstrations. This is when the right has to be balanced against public order and the rights of other citizens to go about their business. Mass picketing during industrial disputes raises similar issues. The law which holds the balance between these conflicting freedoms is now mostly contained in the Public Order Act 1986 which embodies in statutory form with some modifications the common law public order offences of riot, rout, unlawful assembly and affray and also re-enacts and amends the statutory offences dealing with processions and public assemblies previously contained in the Public Order Act 1936.

The Public Order Act 1986, like the Police and Criminal Evidence Act 1984, contains restrictions on the freedom of the individual; it does not state the right of the individual to assemble peacefully. An unsuccessful attempt was made in the House of Lords (HL Deb., vol. 479, col. 436, 24 July 1986) to include a clause in the Bill stating that persons shall be lawfully entitled peacefully to demonstrate or peacefully to hold assemblies. It was rejected by the government partly for the reason that it is a fundamental precept of English law that we are all free to do anything not prohibited by law. However, the government has conceded that it will state the right to assemble and to demonstrate peacefully in a circular about the Act to be sent to police forces which will be published (HC Deb., vol. 96, col. 1069, 30 April 1986), but this will be mere exhortation.

The problem of balancing the freedom to assemble against public order is not a new one. It is epitomized in the old case of *Beatty v. Gillbanks* (1882) where the Salvation Army in Weston-super-Mare were wont to march on a Sunday with a band and banners flying. They were opposed by the Skeleton Army who were antagonistic to their views. Fights ensued and the Salvation Army were told not to march. When they persisted despite being asked by the police to disperse, their leaders were arrested and charged with unlawful assembly. On appeal they were held not guilty because the disturbance of the peace was the fault of their opponents and had not been caused by them. This case was distinguished in the later case of *Duncan v. Jones* (1936) where the facts are closer to the problems of our times. Mrs Duncan wanted to hold a meeting to protest about a repressive Bill, then before Parliament, outside a training centre for the unemployed. On a previous occasion a meeting in the same place addressed by Mrs Duncan had led to disturbances in the training centre. The police asked her to hold the meeting a little distance away; she refused and was arrested. She was convicted of obstructing the police in the execution of their duty. Much ink has been spilt over the attempt to reconcile these cases. This is now merely a matter of historical significance. Under the Public Order Act 1986 the Salvation Army would not be guilty of the offence of violent disorder (section 2) because they did not use or threaten violence nor would they be guilty of the offence of using threatening, abusive or insulting words or behaviour which is intended or likely to cause fear of or to provoke immediate violence (section 4). The law on obstruction of the police has not been changed. More importantly, what the cases illustrate is the eternal difficulty of reconciling freedom of speech and meeting with public order and in consequence the problems of making and applying laws to hold the balance between them. This is particularly true at times of political and economic unrest and it is no coincidence that the first Public Order Act in 1936 was passed because of disturbances resulting from fascist marches and that the second Public Order Act was passed in 1986 in the aftermath of inner city riots, the mass picketing during the miners' strike and mass demonstrations by protest groups.

In view of this it is not surprising that the Public Order Act 1986 tips the balance further in favour of public order and against freedom of meeting. The government recognized in its White Paper preceding the Bill (Cmnd 9510, 1985, para. 1.9) that tightening of the law cannot by itself prevent all disorder and that after disorder has broken out the problem is not a shortage of legal powers but enforcement. This is a matter of practical policing and raises questions of equipment and tactics. More importantly, in the case of large-scale disorders, such as the Brixton and other inner city riots, it raises questions of social policy, particularly towards ethnic minorities, as Lord Scarman stressed in his historic report on the Brixton disorders (Cmnd 8427, 1981, Part VI). It is in the provisions which give the police powers to prevent disorder that the Public Order Act 1986 tips the balance further against the freedom of speech and assembly.

One of the main new provisions in the Act is section 11 which makes it an offence for those organizing a procession to demonstrate for or against a cause or to publicize it or to mark or commemorate an event, not to give six days' advance notice to the police unless this is not reasonably practicable, as in the case of spontaneous demonstrations. This provision is new only in the sense that it applies to the whole country, whereas previous provisions for advance notice only applied in certain areas. It has been argued that the provision is unnecessary as the police usually know in advance about major processions, though this is not so in a minority of cases. The giving of notice is seen as providing a trigger for discussions between the police and the organizers about the manner of conducting the march so as to make the exercise of the statutory powers regulating it unnecessary. On the other hand, where there was no prior knowledge of the march by the police, it would alert them in time to use their powers. It is interesting that a similar provision for static demonstrations and meetings was ruled out by the government for the purely practical reason of generating too much work for the police.

One of the most controversial provisions in the Act was the extension of the powers of the police to impose conditions on a procession (section 12). Though the formal power to give directions imposing conditions which existed under the 1936 Act was rarely used, the existence of the power enables the police to negotiate with the organizers, and the wider the power, the stronger is the bargaining position of the police. The main extension has been in the tests which have to be satisfied before conditions can be imposed. Under the 1936 Act the chief officer of police had to have reasonable grounds for apprehending that the procession might result in serious public disorder. To this the 1986 Act adds reasonable belief of serious damage to property, serious disruption to the life of the community or that the purpose of the organizers is the intimidation of others. These tests widen the power greatly and if used to the full extent could bring almost any large procession within its scope. In theory the exercise of the power could be tested in the courts but in practice the courts have been reluctant to substitute their judgement for that of the police in this area. The conditions which may be imposed are those which appear necessary to the chief constable to prevent disorder, damage, disruption or intimidation, including prescribing the route. It is also now made explicit that conditions can be imposed during the march as well as in advance and the power can then be exercised by the most senior police officer present who could be of junior rank. Failure to comply with a condition knowingly is an offence for the organizers and those taking part and they may be summarily arrested.

Even more controversial has been the extension of this power to impose conditions to public assemblies (section 14). The criteria for the exercise of the power are the same as for processions, and conditions may be imposed as to the place, the duration and the number of persons who may take part. This provision will for the first time give the police a specific statutory power to limit the number of pickets and where they stand, provided that one of the criteria for imposing conditions applies, which in the case of mass picketing would almost certainly be the case. Failure to comply knowingly will be an offence for which one can be summarily arrested. If the powers under this provision were used to the full extent they would enable the police to exercise control over almost any sizeable demonstration. To fall within the provisions the assembly must be of twenty or more people and be held in a public place which is wholly or partly open to the air. This definition carefully excludes private land to which the public is not admitted, and much pressure was brought on the government to extend the Act to trespassers on private land such as the women at Greenham Common or the hippies in the Peace Convoy. At a late stage in the Bill the government finally succumbed to pressure and tabled an amendment to give the police power to direct trespassers to leave land if they reasonably believe that two or more trespassers intend to reside there for any period, that the occupier has taken reasonable steps to get them to leave and that they have caused damage to property or used threatening words or behaviour or have brought twelve or more vehicles on to the land. Failure to obey such a direction or return within three months is a criminal offence (section 39). To make trespass a criminal offence in such circumstances is another major shift in the balance between freedom of the person and public order.

An important distinction between processions and static demonstrations is embodied in the Act in that the power to ban processions (section 13) which is a re-enactment of the provision in the 1936 Act does not apply to public assemblies. The government recognized that meetings and assemblies are a more important means of exercising freedom of speech than marches and that the power to ban would be a major infringement of freedom of speech. The power can only be used where the chief constable reasonably believes that the power to impose conditions on a procession will not be sufficient to prevent serious public disorder. In exercising this power the chief constable must take into account the mutual aid arrangements whereby he can call on assistance from other police forces. He can then apply to the local authority or in London to the Home Secretary for an order banning all processions or a class of procession for up to three months. The order can only be made with the consent of the Home Secretary both in London and elsewhere. There is no power to ban a specific procession because of the danger that this could lead to accusations of political bias. This does, however, mean that, for example, the National Front can stop all other marches by announcing that they will hold a march which as a result of counter-demonstrations is likely to result in serious public disorder. This has happened on a number of occasions and banning orders have increased in the 1980s. Lord Scarman would have liked a power to ban a specific march if there were reasonable grounds for believing that the march was a threat to public order and likely to stir up racial hatred (Cmnd 8427, 1981, para. 7.48). There is no such provision in the 1986 Act which does, however, make the law relating to incitement to racial hatred more effective by giving for the first time a power of summary arrest in such a case (section 18).

The Bill contains no provision for charging the organizers of a demonstration with the cost of policing it. The practical difficulties involved would be very great, but reconciling freedom of speech with public order can be expensive. The estimate for policing demonstrations which required more than a hundred police officers in London in 1984 was nearly £6 million (Cmnd 9510, 1985, para. 6.16).

Probably the most important common law power which the police retain outside the 1986 Act is to prevent imminent breaches of the peace and arrest those responsible. This power was greatly extended during the miners' strike when miners were stopped at a road block on the M1 and were arrested when they tried to proceed. Their conviction for obstructing the police was upheld because on the facts the police acted reasonably in forming the opinion that there was a real risk of a breach of the peace in close proximity both in place and time, there being four pits within five miles of the road block (*Moss v. McLachlan, The Times*, 29 November 1984). That this case was hailed as a limitation on police powers shows how much the police had stretched their powers in setting up other road blocks. The road blocks set up during the industrial dispute at the News International plant at Wapping were justified by the police under the Metropolitan Police Act 1839, section 52 which gives power to direct constables to keep order and prevent obstruction in the immediate neighbourhood of places of public resort and when the streets may be thronged or obstructed. It would again be for the courts to decide whether the Act is being used properly to balance the conflicting freedoms of the residents, the demonstrators and the employers.

A BILL OF RIGHTS

How would the protection of civil liberties be affected if Britain enacted a Bill of Rights based on the European Convention on Human Rights?

Britain is a signatory of this Convention, and individuals such as Malone, who think that their rights under the Convention have been infringed, can bring a petition against the United Kingdom before the European Commission of Human Rights. The Commission may be able to reach a friendly settlement between the parties. If this cannot be achieved, it may refer the case to the European Court of Human Rights consisting of a judge from each country. The judgements of the Court are binding on countries which have signed the Convention but they cannot be enforced. There have been more petitions against the United Kingdom and more have been upheld than against any other signatory which allows individual petitions. They span an enormous range of issues. Apart from the *Malone* case on telephone tapping, they include interrogation methods in Northern Ireland, the closed shop, caning in schools, the immigration rules, the law on homosexuality in Northern Ireland, the abolition of the GLC, the banning of trade unions at GCHQ, the anti-terrorist legislation, the law on contempt, the use of plastic bullets, the rights of prisoners and mental patients, and the law on leasehold reform challenged by the Duke of Westminster. Not all these petitions were successful but a quarter of all the breaches of the Convention found by the Court have been British. British governments have been meticulous in complying with the judgements of the Court, though, as the Interception of Communications Act 1985 shows, this may be the minimum compliance necessary to satisfy the judgement. The procedure for obtaining redress by an individual is slow – it can take five years or more – and legal aid is only available on a limited basis.

Those who support enacting a Bill of Rights into the law of the United Kingdom range from Lord Hailsham to the National Council for Civil Liberties. On several occasions Bills embodying the European Convention have been passed through the House of Lords, the latest occasion being in 1986 supported by Lord Scarman. None of these Bills has so far been acceptable to a British government. The latest Human Rights Bill failed to obtain a second reading in the Home of Commons on 6 February 1987 (HC Deb., vol. 109, col. 1288). These Bills raise fundamental constitutional issues.

The first problem that has to be confronted is the extent to which legal force can be given to the Convention when enacted in an Act of Parliament. The most fundamental rule of the constitution, implicit in the sovereignty of Parliament, is that one Parliament cannot bind its successors. It is, therefore, legally impossible to prevent a future Parliament legislating expressly in contravention of an Act which embodies the Convention. In accordance with the strict interpretation of the doctrine of sovereignty, it is even legally impossible to prevent a future Parliament passing legislation which is inconsistent with the rights under the Convention by implication rather than expressly. In 1986, as on a previous Bill in 1978, the Human Rights Bill had to be amended in the House of Lords to comply with this fundamental rule of the constitution. So far as Acts passed before the Human Rights Bill are concerned, it is, however, possible to provide that they shall only be effective insofar as they do not infringe the rights embodied in the Bill. Also, so far as Acts passed after the enacting of the Human Rights Bill are concerned, it is possible to provide that they shall be construed so as not to infringe the rights there set out except where this is unavoidable in order to give effect to such an Act.

Of more importance than this purely legal issue is the political issue of whether it is desirable that Britain should embody the European Convention into English law rather than merely allow aggrieved individuals to petition the European Commission. The crucial difference would be that the Convention would be binding on British courts and would have to be interpreted by British judges. The rights in the Convention would be enforceable in British courts. Whether this is a good thing or not is a highly controversial question on which there are differences of opinion within the judiciary, the political parties and among constitutional lawyers. Basically the argument turns on whether British judges should be involved in interpreting the very broad terms of the Convention embodying highly politically controversial issues, such as the ones that have been decided by the European Court. The fear is that British judges are not skilled in interpreting broad provisions of this nature and that they would either interpret them legalistically or become involved in political decision-making to a far greater extent than is true currently. The independence of the judiciary from political pressure is one of the cornerstones of the constitution embodied in the Act of Settlement 1701, which provided that judges could only be removed for misbehaviour on an address of both Houses of Parliament. If the judges entered the political arena their impartiality would be much more open to question than at present and governments might be tempted to make political appointments, as is the case with appointments to the Supreme Court in the United States. As we have seen, a British court, unlike the US Supreme Court, would not have the last word in respect of legislation passed by Parliament. Nevertheless the enactment of the European Convention into law would confer considerable political power on an unelected body of persons and constitute an important check on democracy. Whether this is regarded as desirable depends on one's faith in our democratic institutions.

6

Conclusion

We return at the end to the beginning. Why is the British constitution under attack and what, if anything, should be done to reform it? The heart of the problem is what Lord Hailsham called the 'elective dictatorship' – the concentration of power whereby Parliament's power has passed to the Commons and through the party system the power of the Commons became transferred to the Cabinet which has become dominated by the Prime Minister.

The power of the Prime Minister has been increasing. Mrs Thatcher tightened her grip over the Cabinet by steadily eliminating those who did not agree with her policies, and even more importantly by-passing the Cabinet altogether in the case of vital decisions to the extent that charges about the breakdown of constitutional government could be made. The ability of Prime Ministers to assert or set aside collective responsibility is another manifestation of Prime Ministerial power. The ability of a government to survive any defeat in the House of Commons short of a defeat on a motion of confidence can also be seen in this light. Similarly, the resignation of one minister, who becomes the scapegoat for the government as a whole, allows the Prime Minister to survive. Conversely, the Prime Minister can throw the mantle of collective responsibility over an erring minister and thus save him from resignation, though this may not always be politically feasible.

Mrs Thatcher has also tightened her grip on the Civil Service by appointing to the most senior posts those who share her general approach to politics, 'a style of government that values commitment above objectivity' (Treasury Committee Report on Civil Servants and Ministers, HC 92, 1985–6, Evidence, p. 104).

The House of Commons no longer controls the government because of the tight control the government can exercise over MPs in its party through the party whips and the threats and inducements at its command. The vast majority of votes on the floor of the House are, therefore, a foregone conclusion. The House has abdicated all control over the authorization of government expenditure. The opposition can still use its power of delaying Bills to wring some concessions from the government and may occasionally be able to defeat it with the help of rebels from the government side, but this does not apply to the most politically controversial legislation which will be guillotined. Select committees lack even the essential power to make witnesses appear before them against the express wishes of the government, as was demonstrated by the Defence Committee's inability to question the civil servants involved in the Westland affair (HC 519, 1985–6, para. 225 seq.). They have merely reported the matter to the House. The committee did, however, manage to obtain documents which were at first refused (ibid., para. 217 seq.). That a government can survive the condemnations poured on its head by the report of this committee on the government's decision-making relating to Westland is itself symbolic of the strength and weakness of such committees. In a debate on the report the government had a majority of 157 (HC Deb., vol. 103, col. 416, 29 October 1986).

The unreformed House of Lords has little power left. It can be a thorn in the flesh of a Labour government and has recently been so in the case of a Conservative government, but its victories have been minor compared to the volume of government legislation which has been left unscathed.

The power of the government is also vastly increased by giving itself power in statutes to make delegated legislation which is subject to very attenuated parliamentary scrutiny, if at all. This is increasingly being used for matters of policy and principle as well as detail. Even more worrying is the development of quasi-legislation with or without statutory authority which enables the government to make rules of uncertain legal force on matters which Parliament itself would have found difficult to swallow, thus creating back-door legislation.

Ministers also reserve to themselves in Acts of Parliament powers to take individual decisions which they consider too important to entrust to any other body. Where they have entrusted decisions to other bodies such as tribunals, quangos, nationalized industries and local authorities, they still retain considerable powers of appointment to these bodies as well as over their policies. The nationalized industries have been used increasingly as instruments for implementing the government's economic policies, and in the case of local authorities this has led to unprecedented inroads on the autonomy of local government. The sum total of these developments is increased concentration and centralization of power.

This increase in central government power has not been matched by more opportunities for participation in decision-making by those who are most affected by it. Though public inquiries have had their remit broadened to include issues of policy in some cases, this procedure has not satisfied the participants or the government. There are many mechanisms for consultation but the increase in leaks is a symptom of closed government. This is epitomized in the survival of section 2 of the Official Secrets Act 1911 which is almost universally execrated.

There has also been no marked increase in strength in the countervailing control mechanisms or procedures for ensuring public accountability. The courts have been more active in exercising judicial review but this is still very limited both in its scope and numerically – in 1985 there were a thousand applications for judicial review (Woolf, 1986: 222) but this represents only a very small percentage of decisions which are made, and many of the cases have been against local authorities rather than central government. The Ombudsman remains a very shadowy figure who deals with a small number of cases in a limited field which are mostly rather mundane, though very important to the people concerned. The ambit of the Comptroller and Auditor General has not been extended to the nationalized industries or firms in receipt of government subsidies. There has been little development recently in those institutions which would give the consumer a greater say in the provision of services.

Parallel with these developments there has been a considerable extension of police powers both in the Police and Criminal Evidence Act 1984 and the Public Order Act 1986. In the former case the safeguards are not easily enforceable except by the police disciplining themselves. The police have also stretched other powers to deal with major industrial disputes, in particular the miners' strike.

The remedies which have been proposed for these developments fall into two categories. There are those proposals which would make the constitution more democratic, strengthening the elected element and participation by the public. Other proposals would strengthen checks on the elected element by those who are not elected, in particular the judiciary. These different types of proposals are not necessarily inconsistent but may complement each other.

The main proposal to make the constitution more democratic is of course electoral reform. Any system of proportional representation would result in a House of Commons which reflected the votes cast for a particular party more accurately than our present first-past-the-post system. Only in a system where the whole country was counted as one constituency, and seats in the House of Commons were allocated in exact proportion to votes, would the number of seats exactly reflect the votes cast. This system has not been adopted by any country as populous as the United Kingdom and all systems of proportional representation suggested for Britain would not exactly reflect the intentions of the voters, especially if there were a minimum percentage of votes required to obtain a seat, a threshold commonly adopted to exclude very small parties which are sometimes extremist. More importantly, the governments which are most likely to be formed, especially in Britain, if some form of proportional representation were adopted, would be coalitions. The crucial question is with which of the two major parties the third party would ally itself. In Britain it is inconceivable that a coalition would be formed between the Labour and Conservative parties except in time of war or other emergency. It would therefore be up to the Alliance parties to decide with which party they were prepared to form a coalition or at least support, if there were a hung Parliament where no party had an overall majority over all other parties. Unless this was settled before the election, the voter would have no say on this crucial issue and the matter would be settled behind closed doors between the parties concerned. After a coalition has been formed it is also possible for the smallest party to switch allegiance to the opposition, thus putting them into power. This happened in Germany in 1982 when the Free Democratic Party broke away from the Social Democratic Party and joined the Christian Democrats. Thus the smallest party holds the balance of power and can determine which party forms the government and influence its decisions as a member of the coalition. The result is not, therefore, more democratic in that it gives disproportionate power to a minority to determine the composition of the majority. Apart from this, there are problems with the stability of coalitions or pacts, such as the Lib-Lab pact in 1977, which depend on the particular circumstances.

The adoption of proportional representation, which would most probably result in a minority or coalition government, would not at a stroke solve the problem of the elective dictatorship. Only if the coalition falls apart, i.e. if the members of one party no longer support the other partner, will the government be in danger of defeat and there will then have to be a new election, a new coalition or possibly a minority government. The government will, therefore, have to adopt policies to prevent this happening and these will have to be negotiated between the party leaders who will have to carry their parties with them. This is not different in kind from the present situation where the two major parties are also coalitions representing a wide spectrum of views and interests which have to be kept together. The difference is that loyalty within a party tends to be stronger than between parties. It is, therefore, the way the institutions work which is likely to change under a coalition government, rather than the institutions themselves. This could be brought about under the present two-party system.

The relationship between the Prime Minister and the Cabinet would be transformed if Mr Benn's suggestion for the Labour Party that ministers should be elected by the MPs of that party annually were adopted. The Prime Minister would lose the ability to appoint and dismiss ministers which confers enormous power. But even without this radical change, the relationship depends to a large extent on the personalities of those involved. If ministers behave like mice they must expect to be chased, in Mr Callaghan's apt phraseology. Members of the Cabinet should be able collectively to prevent the Cabinet being by-passed on important issues, though pressure of work will necessitate delegation to Cabinet committees. The Cabinet would be strengthened by resuscitation of the Central Policy Review Staff (Think Tank) which was a body of selected civil servants with the addition of secondments from outside the Civil Service who advised the Cabinet as a whole about policy. If decision-making within the Cabinet were more democratic there would be more justification for collective responsibility, and breaches of it by open or covert disagreement should be less frequent. Resignation or dismissal in cases of fundamental disagreement would still be necessary but it is against the spirit of the convention for one minister to be made the scapegoat for the policy of the whole government. The honourable course of action would be for the government as a whole to resign, just as it is the honourable action for a single minister to resign if he has been guilty of conduct unbecoming of a minister, a vague concept but not a meaningless one. To cover up such cases through collective responsibility is to interpret the constitution and constitutional conventions as what can be got away with. It is this cynical attitude to the constitution which, perhaps more than anything else, has discredited it in the eyes of the public.

The obligations of integrity which ministers owe to Parliament and to civil servants have received much consideration in the wake of the Westland and Ponting affairs. The Treasury and Civil Service Committee of the House of Commons which investigated the relationship between ministers and civil servants in the aftermath of these cases recommended that the Prime Minister should, after consultation with the leaders of the other parties in the House of Commons, publish guidelines for ministers setting out their duties to Parliament and their responsibilities for the Civil Service (HC 92, 1985–6, para. 3.13). In their reply the government asserted that it went without saying that ministers' duties and responsibilities to Parliament and in relation to civil servants included obligations of integrity. 'They include the duty to give Parliament and the public as full information as possible about the policies, decisions and actions of the government, and not to deceive or mislead Parliament or the public. In relation to civil servants, they include . . . the duty to refrain from asking or instructing civil servants to do things which they should not do' (Cmnd 9841, para. 11). The reiteration of these obligations of integrity will not prevent another Ponting or Westland affair but it spells out what has hitherto been implicit in the convention of ministerial accountability to Parliament.

As we have seen (Chapter 1), accountability to Parliament no longer involves the resignation of a minister for the acts of civil servants which he has not authorized and of which he was not aware. The Treasury Committee in the light of the Westland affair asked, 'If Crichel Down is dead and ministers are not accountable to Parliament for some actions of their officials, then who is? Not to put too fine a point on it, who ought to resign or to be penalized if mistakes are made? If it is not ministers, it can only be officials' (HC 92, 1985–6, para. 3.17). They thought that a mechanism must be provided to make officials, in cases in which ministers deny responsibility for their actions, accountable to Parliament (ibid., para. 3.19). The government in its reply not surprisingly rejected this as being in conflict with ministerial responsibility (Cmnd 9841, para. 13). But as the Defence Committee in their report on the Westland affair pointed out, 'If ministers cannot demonstrate that officials have behaved properly, the question of disciplinary proceedings arises' (HC 519, 1985–6, para. 237). They then quoted and endorsed the view of the Treasury Committee, 'Whether or not an internal inquiry into various allegations had been made, we understand that no disciplinary action was taken in any case. We are not satisfied that a private internal inquiry which is not fully reported to Parliament constitutes accountability' (ibid., para. 238). Both committees wanted to ensure that where ministers disclaimed responsibility for the acts of civil servants or did not account fully to Parliament, the civil servants were made directly accountable to Parliament through being examined by one of its committees. The government, on the contrary, in their latest guidelines for officials giving evidence to select committees state that it is for ministers alone to investigate the misconduct of civil servants and report to the select committee the results of the inquiry, and not for the officials concerned to be questioned by the committee (Cm 78). The committees have still to accept this.

The situation was reversed in the case of Mr Ponting who appealed to this same principle of direct accountability to Parliament by civil servants where ministers have not discharged their responsibility to Parliament. But the Treasury Committee disapproved of Mr Ponting's behaviour, though they sympathized with his predicament (HC 92, 1985–6, Part IV). They recommended a more expanded note of guidance for civil servants and a right of appeal by the civil servant to the Head of the Civil Service where the dilemma could not be resolved. The government has accepted this latter recommendation (Cmnd 9841, para. 19).

The Treasury Committee found no evidence of the politicization of the Civil Service in the sense that senior appointments were made on the basis of political affiliations. However, they approved of the appointment of senior civil servants who were in tune with the government's policy, though they recognized that this had long-term implications for a non-political Civil Service and that this approach has met with strong opposition. They were not in favour of a politicized Civil Service but they wanted the minister's capacity to implement his policies strengthened by expanding his private office with more political advisers and his parliamentary private secretary, who would be there to keep the minister in touch with backbench MPs (HC 92, 1985–6, Part V). The government gave a lukewarm welcome to such ministerial policy units (Cmnd 9841, para. 30 seq.).

The key to the elective dictatorship lies in the fact that the government controls Parliament and not Parliament the government. The remedy for this can only lie in the hands of MPs themselves. If MPs do not use their votes they only have themselves to blame. If MPs voted by secret ballot, at least on some issues, they would find it easier to vote against their party but this is unlikely to be conceded by any political party. Even under the present system it would be possible for MPs to challenge government expenditure more effectively by using existing procedures, and if MPs backed up the recommendations of their own select committees on the floor of the House this would alter the balance of power between the government and Parliament.

Reform of the House of Lords has so far proved impossible. If it became more democratic by making it a wholly or partially elected House, it would become a rival to the House of Commons and stalemate could ensue. If the House of Lords were reformed on the lines proposed in 1968 by the creation of more life peers, it would increase even further the power of patronage of the Prime Minister.

The use of delegated legislation for issues of policy and principle could be monitored by Parliament and subjected to greater scrutiny. It would also be possible to improve parliamentary scrutiny over delegated legislation by making the procedure in standing committees considering such instruments more effective and devising a procedure for amendment. There is also a need for Parliament to monitor and scrutinize more closely the increasing use of codes of practice and guidelines whose legal effect is uncertain.

The great increase in the centralization of power would be reversed if proposals for devolution to the countries and regions of the United Kingdom were adopted by a future government. Less drastic proposals for restructuring local government would give more power and autonomy to the only directly elected public authorities apart from the House of Commons.

There is more opportunity for the ordinary citizen to participate in decision-making at the local level than at the level of central government. This can take many forms but most commonly involves consultation and the ability to voice one's opinions. This could be enhanced by further strengthening of grass roots democracy through institutions like neighbourhood councils and by strengthening the voice of the consumer vis-à-vis the nationalized industries and the National Health Service. At the level of central government the climate would be transformed towards open government if section 2 of the Official Secrets Act 1911 were repealed and a Freedom of Information Act passed.

Referenda, which in theory are the most democratic form of decision-making, have been used on two occasions by Labour governments, in 1975 on the decision of whether to remain in the EEC and in 1979 on devolution to Scotland and Wales. They were both issues on which there were deep divisions within the Labour Party, and the government could be said to have been appealing to the people in order to heal this split. Referenda are a form of direct democracy which requires a great deal of faith in democracy in its purest form.

At the opposite end of the spectrum are proposals for enacting a Bill of Rights to enhance the power of the courts to safeguard the rights of the individual by testing any infringement against the broad provisions of a statute embodying the European Convention on Human Rights. This proposal would provide a check on democracy as it would confer much greater power on the courts to construe Acts of Parliament. Under our present constitution, the sovereignty of Parliament would ensure that Parliament had the last word, but

Lord Hailsham (1976) went further to propose the enactment of a new constitution under which Parliament would no longer be sovereign and which could only be altered by a special procedure such as that contained in the United States constitution. Such a proposal is not within the realm of practical politics.

Within our existing constitution fundamental changes to combat the elective dictatorship can be made, such as electoral reform, devolution and the enactment of a Bill of Rights. The first could transform the functioning of government, the second would decentralize decision-making and the last would increase the power of the judiciary. Each would have important repercussions: electoral reform on the stability of governments, devolution on the unity of the United Kingdom and a Bill of Rights on the non-political status of the judiciary. Without these fundamental reforms, the climate could be changed from an elective dictatorship to a participatory democracy without any alterations in the law, if those elected to power behaved differently. If ministers did not allow themselves to be dominated by the Prime Minister, if MPs used their votes and if decisions were reached whenever possible by consensus after taking into account the views of those affected, the nature of our democracy would be transformed. This would probably not affect the economic performance of the United Kingdom but it should prevent the constitution being blamed for the faults of those who exercise power. A democracy is only as good as the people who are elected as its representatives.

Bibliography

Bagehot, W. (1963), *The English Constitution* (first edition 1867), London: Fontana.

Bell, K. (1975), *Research Study on Supplementary Benefit Appeal Tribunals*, London: HMSO.

Benn, A. (1980), 'The Case for a Constitutional Premiership', *Parliamentary Affairs*, p. 7.

Boyle, Lord (1980), 'Ministers and the Administrative Process', *Public Administration*, p. 1.

Crossman, R. (1975), *The Diaries of a Cabinet Minister*, London: Jonathan Cape.

Dicey, A. V. (1939), *Law of the Constitution* (first edition 1885), London: Macmillan.

Finer, S. E. (1956), 'Individual Responsibility of Ministers', *Public Administration*, p. 377.

Ganz, G. (1974), *Administrative Procedures*, London: Sweet and Maxwell.

Hailsham, Lord (1976), 'Elective Dictatorship', *Listener*, 21 October.

Harlow, C. and Rawlings, R., (1984), *Law and Administration*, London: Weidenfeld and Nicolson.

Jenkins, R. (1979), 'Home Thoughts from Abroad', *Listener*, 29 November.

Mackintosh, J. (1977), *The British Cabinet*, third edition, London: Sweet and Maxwell.

National Economic Development Office (1976), *A Study of U. K. Nationalised Industries*, London: HMSO.

Norton, P. (1982), *The Constitution in Flux*, Oxford: Martin Robertson.

Outer Circle Policy Unit (1979), *The Big Public Inquiry*, London: Outer Circle Policy Unit.

Scarman, Lord (1985), 'The Shifting State, Public Administration in a Time of Change', *Public Administration*, p. 1.

Shell, D. (1985), 'The House of Lords and the Thatcher Government', *Parliamentary Affairs*, p. 16.

Wass, Sir D. (1983), *The Reith Lectures*, London: BBC.

Woolf, Sir H. (1986), 'Public Law – Private Law: Why the Divide?', *Public Law*, p. 220.

Cases

Numbers in bold refer to pages in the text

Index

121

Index

UNDERSTANDING
EQUITY AND TRUSTS

Jeffrey Hackney

Understanding Equity and Trusts seeks to reveal the arguments and reasons underlying this particular aspect of the law, and to encourage the reader to participate in evaluating them.

The Equity jurisdiction, which takes its name from the first principle of justice, began as discretionary intervention, supporting, supplementing and correcting the more ancient common law. It has become a separate system, with its own doctrines and remedies, and dominated by its most substantial and characteristic contribution to the legal system of which it is a part, the trust, which is first and foremost a property-management device of great sophistication, versatility and beauty. This creature has been successfully transformed from its ancient feudal origins to a flourishing commercial mechanism which is a mainstay of every contemporary pension fund manager and tax planner.

Jeffrey Hackney exposes the essential shape and nature of the trust, looking at its social uses and at the wide variety of arrangements and conclusions which pass under its name. His approach is thematic, describing the patterns and the doctrines which underpin the detailed decisions. This is a critical book, assessing from a standpoint of warm admiration the common law's most glorious failure. Written with the minimum of citation, his book transforms an area of law often regarded as arid into one full of life.

UNDERSTANDING TORT LAW

Carol Harlow

Tort law is the technical name for part of our system of civil liability. When people turn to the legal system for compensation for some injury which they have suffered, the rules of tort law come into play. So tort law has to deal with a wide range of situations. If a careless driver causes an accident, for example, he may be legally liable and he (or more often his insurers) will have to compensate those who have been injured. In a very different case, a householder whose neighbours disturb him by their noise or other annoying habits may want the nuisance ended. He, too, can turn to tort law. So could someone whose reputation has been damaged by a defamatory article in a newspaper. To deal with these disparate situations, tort law needs to be versatile and to keep in tune with changing social needs.

Understanding Tort Law sets out to place the modern rules of tort into their social context in order to help those who are new to the subject to follow its development. It outlines the way in which the rules are made and describes their origins in a very different society. The book also provides a simple introduction to tort law's complex and confusing rules and technical vocabulary.

UNDERSTANDING CRIMINAL LAW

C. M. V. Clarkson

The main focus of *Understanding Criminal Law* is on the general principles of criminal liability and the most important offences – homicide and the other crimes against the person, sexual offences, and the various property offences such as theft and burglary. It explains the substantive rules of criminal law within the context of the law's overall objectives, showing that the distinction between murder and manslaughter, for instance, can be properly understood only if the law's purpose is also appreciated. In doing this, the rationale of the various rules and the relationship between them is explored. This examination reveals that the criminal law is concerned with protecting certain values. The author exposes these values and subjects them to scrutiny, at times expressing preferences as to how the criminal law should develop. His book presents a straightforward and stimulating approach to understanding criminal law.